A *Very* Practical Guide to Discipline with Young Children

A *Very* Practical Guide to Discipline with Young Children

by
Dr. Grace L. Mitchell

Telshare Publishing, Inc. • *1982*

International Standard Book Number 0–910287–00–7

Library of Congress Cataloging in Publication Data

Mitchell, Grace L.
  A very practical guide to discipline with young children.

  Includes index.
  1. Discipline of children. I. Title.
HQ770.4.M57 1982   649'.64   82-16951
ISBN 0-910287-00-7

Fifth printing

Illustrations by Sylvia Feinburg

Table of Contents

Dedication ix

Acknowledgments xi

Foreword xv

Introduction—IAM! I CAN! A Philosophy That Works! xvii

Chapter 1: Parents Are Teachers 1

Definition of Discipline 2
What Will "They" Think? 5
A Fourstep Plan for Action 6

Chapter 2: ANTICIPATE and Avoid Trouble 7

Operating on More Than One Channel 9
What Are Your Zero Hours? 10

Chapter 3: HESITATE Before You Act 15

Chapter 4: INVESTIGATE the Cause 19

Seeking Clues to Behavior 19

Chapter 5: COMMUNICATE—Open the Doors of Understanding 25

Pouring Fuel on the Flames 27

Chapter 6: Basic Trust 33

Trust Is The "Core" of Relationships 34
Parents Are Not Always Perfect 34
Child Abuse Isn't Always Physical 35

Chapter 7: Doing What Comes Naturally   37

Eating   38
A Touch of Class   39
Table Manners   41
Mealtime in the Child Care Center   41
You Can't Win!   43
Eliminating   43
Sleeping   43
Dressing   45
A Sense of Order   47

Chapter 8: Behavior That Bugs You   49

Biting   49
Lying   54
Truth is Stranger Than Fiction   55
Why Do They Tell Lies?   57
Stealing   59
Unacceptable Language   60
Bathroom Talk   62
Throwing   65
Temper Tantrums   67

Chapter 9: Move Over for The New Baby   71

How Would You Feel?   72
Delayed Feelings of Jealousy   73
Covering Up Jealousy   75
Make the Child a Part of the Planning   77

Chapter 10: Grown-Ups Goof Too!   81

Making Threats You Can't Carry Out   81
Offering Choices When There Are No Choices   84
The "Put Down" Destroys the "I AM"   86
Comparison and Competition   88
Bribes and Rewards   90
Gold Stars   91

Contents

Demanding Apologies   91
Nagging and Scolding   96

Chapter 11: Call In the Reserves   99

Teachers and Parents Understand Each Other   103
Don't Try to "Wing It" Alone   103

Chapter 12: Some Thoughts on Punishment   105

What Are Your "Or Elses"?   105
Spanking   106
Wearing Two Hats   109
Isolation and Separation   113
The "Thinking Chair"   114

Chapter 13: An Ounce of Prevention   117

Bring the Feelings Out in the Open   118
The Pressure Cooker   119
Dictating Stories and Poems   120
Puppets   121
Pounding   126
Painting Is More Than Art   127
Waterplay—The Most Accessible Material   129
Reading and Telling Stories   129
Music   131
Dramatic Play Discloses Feelings   132

Chapter 14: A Piece of the Action   135

"The Wallace Corporation"—A Family Meeting   135
Allowances   138
Democracy in the Classroom   140
Honest Listening   142
"Talk—It—Over" Chairs   143
Tape Recorders   144

Chapter 15: Wrong Way! Turn Back!   147

  A Plan for Change   148
  Look at Your Own "I AM"   148
  How Were You Disciplined?   149
  *What Kind of Adults Do You Want Your
    Children to Be?*   150
  It's Later Than You Think!   151

Chapter 16: In A Nutshell   153

Index   155

About the Author   161

To Rosalie Richardson

A dedicated teacher of "special children" who taught us that all children are special. Her creative ideas for helping children to reach for their full potential, and her keen sense of humor are reflected in many of the stories in this book.

Acknowledgments

Writing this book turned out to be a bittersweet experience. The pages are crowded with images of the people who influenced me over the years; friends; colleagues in the teaching profession, parents and children. In passing on what I learned from them I feel that I am, in a sense, paying my dues.

I see the stern but kind faces of Alice Mifflin, Eleanor Clark and Abigail Eliot and guiltily wonder whether I have lived up to the high standards they exemplified.

Like warm encircling arms I sense the presence of Ruth Stone and Bertha Forster, each of whom had a special gift for making me aware of my shortcomings without preaching or inflicting pain. I am indebted to Louise Barnicle, Helen Peterson, and Virginia Thayer who helped me set the cornerstones of the Green Acres Day School in place, and to George and Al Naddaff who stretched my educational bias to encompass the additional advantages of sound business practices.

My own three children returned everything I ever invested in them one hundred fold, but it is the hundreds and thousands of children whose lives were shared with me in preschool and day camp who were my best teachers. They dance across the screen of my memory, peer shyly around corners or blow through my mind like a warm zephyr.

To the people who took the time to read my manuscript and offer helpful comments and suggestions, I am eternally grateful.

Karen Zappe, Director of Training, Children's World, Evergreen, Colorado

Sylvia Feinburg, Department of Early Childhood Education, Tufts University, Medford, Massachusetts

Judith Comjean, Director, Green Acres Day School, Waltham, Massachusetts

Cynthia Wallace, Director, The Children's Centre, Londonderry, New Hampshire

Christa and Matty Tumbiolo, parents of Matthew, five, and Ashley, seven months.

Darlene and Gardner Garrett, parents of Carl, eight, and Vicky, six.

Margo Childs, Vykki Dewsnap and Nancy Archiprete adjusted their own busy schedules to accommodate my typing needs, Edna Adams and Linda Bailey fed the manuscript into the computer which regurgitated finished copies, and Mary Mindess, Director of Early Childhood Education at Lesley College took over the specialized task of indexing.

My sister, Lois Dewsnap, worked closely with me from start to finish, discussing the cases we selected to illustrate the problems, contributing stories from her own twenty years of teaching experience, and combing the contents with an editor's fine tooth comb.

In this, as in every project I undertake, my husband, Donald Mitchell, has been patiently accompanying me — waiting for me — and listening when I needed a sounding board.

"Discipline is the slow, bit by bit, time consuming task of helping children to see the sense in acting in a certain way."

Dr. James Hymes

Foreword

This book is addressed to parents, teachers, grandparents, indeed everyone who is living with or working with young children, between the ages of two and eight.

It is based on more than half a century of experience as a teacher, mother and grandmother, and embellished with true stories from one who has made most of the mistakes, fretted through many of the frustrations, and smiled with the successes. My stories have an emotional content—they deal with the feelings which come pouring out of my memories. Living and learning with children is a growth experience, an education in the skills of human relationships. If we will but listen to our children, and try to understand what they are telling us through their behavior, which is their second language, we can learn from them. I do not believe that children are born bad, or annoying, or obnoxious. It is what the world does to them which shapes their personalities.

Each of my stories has a small lesson. Each reader will interpret them from his own perspective; my goal is to increase the scope of that perspective; to open up new avenues of thought—and offer options for action!

If I am successful you will find a new measure of joy in living and learning with YOUR children!

Introduction

I AM! I CAN! A Philosophy That Works!

INTELLECTUAL

PHYSICAL

EMOTIONAL

SOCIAL

There is a basic philosophy which undergirds everything I think, teach, preach, and follow in my daily life. It can be stated in four short words, "I AM!" "I CAN!" It is a part of me; I have assimilated it. It begins with the phrase from The Bible, "Love thy neighbor as thyself." I was well into my thirties before I really understood that verse. It always seemed as if we should concentrate on loving our neighbors—that there was something immoral about self love. The light broke through when I finally came to realize that you are incapable of loving your neighbor *until* you feel good about yourself. When you really love another you have a desire to contribute to that person's well being, either in a material way or psychologically. True—you can offer the proverbial chicken soup—but the giver with a weak "I AM" will even have to dilute that with, "It's not my best. The chicken wasn't as good as usual. I cooked it too long. It needs something!"

A gloomy, pessimistic, self-deprecating individual whose major talent lies in rendering apologies is unable to offer sympathy, encouragement, praise or confidence to his neighbors.

George Naddaff, my partner and co-founder of the Living and Learning Day Care Centers, said to me one day, "Grace, what do you want for children?"

As I answered him I drew the above sketch, explaining as I went along.

"The square represents a human being," I said, "one who is growing, developing, changing from the moment of his birth in four ways. Physically as bones and muscles develop; socially as a member of an ever-enlarging community; intellectually as the computer in his brain takes in and spits out more information; and emotionally as he is learning to cope with the strains and stresses encountered in everyday life.

The child who comes to nursery school is like the jagged pieces of rock that break away from the ledge out in the ocean in front of my home. These pieces wash ashore where, with every tide, they roll against other stones. (The sound of this constant rubbing lulls me to sleep at night when the sea is in a gentle mood and echoes with a roar when a nor'easter blows in.) I can go down to my beach and pick up stones that are almost perfectly round and so smooth to touch that it is a pleasurable sensation to handle them. I can also see some newly arrived stones in the process of becoming smooth, and I compare them to the little children who are also in the stage of "becoming." A young man, on his first real job, was resentful of his boss. "He's picking on me!" he sputtered. "Every little mistake I make is a big deal! I'm quitting! He rubs me the wrong way!"

"He isn't rubbing you the wrong way," a friend remarked. "He's just rubbing you smooth!"

As parents and teachers of young children we have been given the privilege of "rubbing young children smooth." We don't have to use a harsh sandpaper, a gentle polishing with a soft cloth will achieve better results.

Within the square of development I have a circle which represents the individual after the sharp points have been smoothed. That circle can *never* be perfectly round. If it were, it would suggest a perfect person, one who was physically superior, socially well adjusted, intellectually brilliant and always emotionally stable; a person who looked like a smooth round peg fitting neatly into a smooth round hole. A world filled with round pegs would be utterly boring; it is because we are all uniquely put together that we each have something to contribute. We need leaders who have the intelligence, imagination and ability to get us on the moon, but we also need the workers who make it possible. The man who makes the tiniest part of the rocket ship can be as important as the winner of the Nobel Prize. There is a niche—a place in the sun—for each one of us!

When the "I AM" is strong—when a person feels good about himself, self confidence allows him to venture, to take risks, and to attempt new feats, whether it be the infant taking his first step, or the mountain climber. If he reaches his goal, his "I CAN" expands.

"I did it! I did it! I DID IT!" I shouted, and wrote to all of my friends when I earned my Ph.D. I know what it means to have your "I AM" stretch and grow; and I have discovered that with each achievement a new door opens to another exciting new experience. The "I AM" feeds the "I CAN", which in turn reinforces the "I AM" and a positive circular motion falls into place.

These two concepts — the four areas of development and the "I AM! I CAN!" have become measuring sticks for me. They apply to the members of my family, to people who work for and with me, and to children whose lives I am able to touch directly or through others.

I use these yardsticks when I select staff people to work in child care. Certainly it is essential that they have physical stamina — working in a child care center is HARD; certainly they must be able to get along well with their colleagues, and with the parents of the children they are caring for. I believe that true intelligence means knowing what you don't know, and so I look for people who are eager to grow in their profession; who have plans for continuing growth, and last, but far from least, people who are emotionally strong enough to maintain their cool when operating under stressful conditions.

I use this measuring stick when I purchase a new piece of equipment. It must offer oportunities for development in at least three of those four areas for me to be willing to invest in it.

Teachers and parents who are in daily contact with children need to be constantly aware of the subtle ways in which they can influence the positive motion of the "I AM, I CAN" and to be conscious also of the subtle ways in which they can put that motion in reverse.

They do it with the put down: "How stupid can you get?" Humiliation: "So you can wear diapers until you can act like a big girl."

They do it with rejection — "Walk behind me. I don't want anyone to know such a scruffy looking kid belongs to me," and with all the cruel, hurtful things adults say which make a child feel "I'm no good! I can't do anything right!" Ugly words can set that motion spinning in the wrong direction.

So that is my platform! The "I AM, I CAN" philosophy works! You can call it self-confidence, or competency, you can talk about positive and negative reinforcement—or whatever words you choose—but the theory remains constant. The most important thing you can do for your own child, or a student, is to help him hold his head high—"I AM!"—reach out for the stars—"I CAN!"—and know the sweet satisfaction of success!

A *Very* Practical
Guide to Discipline
with Young Children

CHAPTER 1

PARENTS ARE TEACHERS

What are the words that pop into your mind when you think of Discipline?

Obedience? Punishment? Making kids mind?

How often we hear people say, "That kid is spoiled.... His parents never discipline him."

"He wouldn't be such a brat if he got a little discipline."

"That teacher has poor discipline. Her kids walk all over her."

"Kids today don't know the meaning of discipline."

For most people the word discipline has a negative connotation. It implies that someone is going to tighten the thumb screws. Parents or teachers are obligated to *do* something to a child. The law and courts *do* something to recalcitrant adults.

What I propose here is a plan of action for dealing with behavior which will ultimately lead to *self-discipline.* My plan presupposes that the adults who try to follow it in their dealings with young children will, themselves, have achieved some measure of self-discipline. It also makes the assumption that from the moment of birth a child is a thinking, feeling, human being, and that our task is to *help* him develop into a competent, self-confident adult. To that end, I have chosen a definition which puts the adult in the role of advisor and helper, ready to step in and rescue the child from mistakes which will harm him physically or emotionally, but willing to let him make the mistakes which will enable him to grow. This definition is so much the core of everything that follows that I toyed with the idea of printing it at the top of every page! I will, instead, make

1

frequent references to it. Here, then, is the heart of my beliefs:

> Discipline is the slow, bit-by-bit, time consuming task of helping children see the *sense* in acting in a certain way.

I'LL TEACH YOU!

"Bus 135 — N.Y. to Boston — leaving at Station 6!"

When the announcement came over the speaker, the young mother wearily picked up her suitcase and grasped her two-year-old by the hand. Her four-year-old son was carrying a shopping bag bulging with sweaters, coloring books and crayons, small cars, and other paraphernalia while his sister struggled with a stuffed rabbit which was her equal in size.

"Go on, Sam," Zelda urged, prodding him from behind. "Hurry up. People are waiting to get on."

"I want to sit by the window," Molly whined, as Sam hustled into that favored spot.

"No way!" he grinned. "I got here first!"

Molly set up a howl and Zelda sat down and pulled her onto her lap. "Shhh!" she said, soothingly, "You will have a turn later. We have a long time to be on this bus."

As they left the city the children were busy looking out the window. When they began to get restless, Zelda brought forth the coloring books and settled down to read a magazine, hoping for a breather — but it was not to be.

"I have to pee," Sammy announced in a loud voice.

"Me, too!" Molly was quick to follow.

"You just went in the bus station," Zelda whispered. "It's too soon to go again."

"But I have to!" Sammy wailed, jumping up and down. "I'm going to wet my pants!"

Zelda, her face flushed with embarrassment, started down the aisle to the lavatory at the rear of the bus, pushing Sammy ahead of her again and carrying Molly. The children beamed and smiled at the passengers, obviously ready to respond to any friendly overture.

When they were back in their seats, Zelda tried once more to read. Molly had the window seat this time. For a few minutes all was quiet, and then the argument began again.

"Molly's had the window for a long time! It's my turn now!"

"It is not! You had it longer!"

"Here, Sam, why don't you read this book to Molly?" Zelda said, as she handed him a story book.

"No, I don't wanna," Sam answered, sulkily.

"Yes you do. I wanna hear it," Molly whined, whereupon Sam used the book to whack Molly on the head.

Her frustration blew the lid right off Zelda's tolerance. "I'll teach you to hit people," she screamed, as she slapped Sammy in the face!

AND SHE DID!

How does this story make you feel? Does Zelda's lack of control shock you? Does it dredge up guilty memories of times when you have shown a similar display of temper?

I first heard the story when I was attending a conference for pre-school teachers in 1946. Dr. Lawrence Frank, a well-known educator and author, described it as an incident he had witnessed.

Those words "I'll teach you to hit people!" were indelibly etched on my mind and from that day have flashed warning signals when I have been on the verge of *teaching* the wrong behavior through my own actions. At such times I can see him standing there on the stage, his kindly face, topped with a shock of white hair, and I hear him say — in a dramatically quiet tone,

"And she did!"

How often do we as parents and teachers *teach* our children to do the very things we punish them for? We yell or shout at them in angry tones and then we scold them for engaging in shouting matches with their peers. We criticize them, embarrass and humiliate them in front of others as if they were robots instead of feeling, human beings, but we are outraged when they indulge in name calling, hurt their friends with such labels as "Fatso", or "Dummy" or resort to racial slurs and name calling.

With the best intentions we allow ourselves to attack children verbally — and even physically — when, if we could all have a warning signal which flashes automatically, if that signal had been thoroughly assimilated into our mindset, it might serve as a brake when our emotions take precedence over reason.

In our frustration we are all reaching for definite answers. This is the age of the written word. There are "how to" books on every conceivable subject. A publisher recently told me that the two most popular are cookbooks and books on discipline, and it occurred to me that if someone were clever enough to combine the two subjects, it might turn out to be a best seller! If I want to make an apple dumpling I can go to my favorite cookbook and find a recipe. Parents would love to be able to thumb through the index of a book and find a sure-fire recipe for dealing with fighting, lying, or temper tantrums! Teachers who are stumped when faced with defiant, aggressive, foul-mouthed kids would be grateful for tried and true formulas that would enable them to maintain control of their classrooms! Unfortunately there can never be cookbook recipes for dealing with human behavior because the ingredients will never be the same in any two situations. Each incident will be the result of a combination of people with unique personalities, the environment in which it takes place, and the immediate circumstances. These ingredients are stable but they will never be measured out in the same amounts and so the product, in the case of discipline, is unpredictable. The thread of consistency which can meld them together is the definition we have chosen. If our goal is clear and if the ultimate product we seek is a child who has learned *self-discipline* we will not turn out look-alike products but we can find some joy and satisfaction in the process of turning out confident, competent individuals.

There is one thing parents and teachers have in common, which is also their greatest asset. Whether they deserve it or not and whether they like it or not, they wear the halos of heroes. Every child really wants to bask in the sunshine of approval of a favored adult. At home it is one or both parents; in school it is the teacher.

The word "discipline" stems from "disciple" and a disciple is one who identifies with his leader, and who consciously tries to follow in his footsteps. The leaders in a child's world are his parents and his teachers. A child *needs* to look up to his parents, for they represent his only security in a world which can be very frightening. We hear the little boy boasting, "My father is BIG!" "My father is strong—he can fight anyone!" "My father is so smart—he knows!" and even though father looks like Caspar Milquetoast, he is a hero in his child's eyes.

On the other hand, we have only to observe children playing school at home to recognize that they copy their teacher's mannerisms and tone of voice.

Living up to such admiration places an awesome responsibility on all of us—but at the same time it gives us an advantage. If we can believe that down deep the child wants to please us, we may be able to transcend the immediate natural reaction we feel when we are on the receiving end of a well-placed kick in the shins or a torrent of four-letter words, and act like mature adults instead of unequally matched antagonists. If we can rise to a level where in our minds we are asking, "What can be going on in the life of this child which makes him want to lash out at the world?" we may be able to look for reasons behind the behavior. At that point we will be on our way toward making the definition work.

What Will "They" Think?

The innate desire of the child to win approval is a positive asset we share. On the negative side we share a common fear. We are all concerned about what "THEY" think of us. Like the phrase "I'll teach you..." there has been another sentence which has been reiterated through the years in my own family. Back in the days when my children were old enough to be helping as counselors or aides in my day camp we had a psychologist come to a pre-camp training session to talk about discipline. The speaker, Dr. Volta Hall, said, "I was nagging my son because he wouldn't get a haircut and I heard myself saying 'What will the neighbors think of *me*?'"

On more than one occasion after that when I was scolding about some trivia, one of my children would point a finger at me and say, in exaggerated tones, "What will the neighbors think of ME?" I believe we all fall into this trap at some time. Particularly now, when so many mothers are working outside the home, it is easy to imagine that friends, neighbors, relatives (especially in-laws) are critical behind our backs. We read disapproval into every casual remark, and our anxiety stands in the way of common sense.

Throughout this book, you will find constant references to three main themes: our definition, the inescapable fact that parents are role models for their children's behavior; and the encouraging thought that a major factor in discipline is the use of common sense!

A Fourstep Plan for Action

In the coming chapters I propose to substitute positive action for reliance on the old ways of nagging, scolding, yelling at children and punishing them.

The key words in my four-point plan of action are: **ANTICI-PATE, HESITATE, INVESTIGATE,** and **COMMUNICATE.**

These four mandates cannot be separated into neat compartments. In some of the anecdotes that follow, one is more obvious than another, but usually they are all present to some extent. As you read, you will find them mentioned again and again, and each time they will bring new insights to your own understanding of the goals of discipline.

CHAPTER 2

Anticipate and Avoid Trouble

As Mrs. Thomas pulled into the driveway, she noticed that her son's car was in the other side of the garage. David is home early, she thought, then glanced at her watch and realized that she was late. She set her bag of groceries on the kitchen table, and went through to the living room. Her cheerful greeting died on her lips when she saw her son, lying on the couch, staring despondently at the ceiling.

"What's wrong?" she asked anxiously.

David sat up and forced a smile, "Nothing for you to be alarmed about. I've just had a lousy day with my kids and I am doing some serious thinking; I am wondering whether this is the right career for me. I like the work, and sometimes I think I am a darned good teacher and then on a day like today I think I am not doing these kids much good, and they sure don't do anything for my ego!"

Mrs. Thomas sank into her favorite easy chair and kicked off her shoes. "Tell me about it," she invited as she massaged one foot with the toes of the other. "Was it one special incident or the whole day?"

Her tall, rangy son stood up and walked around the room as he talked. "Well, it really began at snack time," he said. "We had a good morning up till then. That old briefcase I took in set up a whole new chain of activities. They set up an office near the housekeeping corner and were really involved in dramatic play. And then when we were at the table we had great conversation. But when we were through, I said, 'O.K., now we are going out on the playground' and you would think I had pushed a button that set off a cyclone. They all jumped up and made a mad dash for the door. Kenny bumped into Jacques who turned around and punched him, yelling, 'You knocked me down, you dummy!' Of course Kenny hit back, and then some of the other kids got into it and all of a sudden I had a first rate fight on my hands. A couple of little girls got scared and began to cry—and just at that moment Liz (the director) walked in with a visitor. I got the kids together as fast as I could and took them outside. Liz left early so I didn't hear about it today, but I expect I will tomorrow when we have our conference."

Mrs. Thomas smiled sympathetically. "That was this morning. Was the rest of the day so bad?"

"Yeah, that's where my doubts come in. I should have been able to get things back under control, but it seems as if they were out to get me for the rest of the day. Three kids spilled their milk at lunch; I had a hassle with that new kid, Jason—he called me a fancy four-letter name when I told him to clean up the mess he had made. No one slept at rest and I lost my patience and yelled at them! The whole afternoon just seemed to tell me I am not temperamentally suited to work with little kids. They are learning all the wrong things from me!"

Mrs. Thomas continued with what seemed to be an irrelevant question. "Does the school have a plan for evacuating the children in case of fire?"

David looked at her—startled and somewhat annoyed. "Of course!"

"Do you have fire drills to test your plan?"

"Certainly!"

"Well, someone had to think that plan out from beginning to end, **ANTICIPATE** all of the possible dangers, and then test them. Now let's go back and look at the incident that gave you so much grief and see what kind of planning you could have done.

"Remember, you have only been a full-fledged teacher for two months. When you were in training there was always someone standing by to pull your chestnuts out of the fire. By now I guess you know that your real education began *after* you graduated, and began to put all that book learning into practice! As a former teacher I have news for you. The learning process

Plan ahead for what could happen or to avoid what could happen

never stops! When you work with growing, living, human beings they will continue to teach you as much as you teach them! Some of it adds up to plain common sense but most of it is through trial and error."

"I can agree with your theory," David retorted, "but I thought you were going to tell me what I did that was wrong."

"I intend to try," she responded with a smile. "It sounds as if you failed to **ANTICIPATE**."

Operating on More Than One Channel

"What do you mean by that?" he asked, with a thoughtful frown.

"You have an eight track tape in your car," Mrs. Thomas went on. "Your brain may not be ready to function on eight tracks now, but it certainly can operate on more than one. For example, while you were still sitting at the table that second track should have been saying 'When we finish with our snack we are going outside. How am I going to move this group of kids from here to there in an orderly fashion?'

"Then you could have quietly and matter-of-factly said 'In a few minutes when everyone is through, we are going outside. First I need two helpers to clean up the table. Jan and Jerry, you may do it today. Be sure to get the dustpan and brush and sweep up the crumbs under the table and take a sponge and wipe the table top. Joe, you pick up the cups and put them into the waste basket, and Sally, you may take the cracker basket back to the kitchen. The rest of us are going to get our jackets. Now all the people who have something blue on may go first.

"Making an orderly transition from one activity to another is an acquired skill," she went on, "but when you learn it, your problems with group management will be greatly diminished. When you abruptly say, 'We are going out' with no forewarning, you are practically inviting them to stampede!"

"I see what you mean," David grinned, feeling better already. "Did you learn all that when you were a teacher? Seems to me that you practiced some of it when we were kids. Can you really think on two tracks simultaneously?"

"Sure," she said, "I do it all the time. I suspect that you do, too. You just haven't been aware of it. As to when you were little, yes, I had to learn to plan ahead. For instance, if I said at the breakfast table, 'I think we will go to the beach today', you might not have knocked me over on your way out the door, but I would have found myself with a table full of dirty dishes. Instead I would give out the directions.

"'David will clear the table and load the dishwasher.'

"'Sally can mix up some tuna salad and make sandwiches.'

"'Dan, you make a gallon of lemonade, and when you have all made your beds and finished your jobs, we will take off!'"

David laughed delightedly. "Of course! I remember those assignments, but I didn't realize then that you were manipulating us. You're really something, Mum! Thanks for the tip. I can't wait now to get back to the center to try it out!"

I have heard it said that no one ever uses more than ten percent of his innate human potential. I truly believe that everyone *can* operate on more than one channel at the same time. I suspect some brilliant minds can keep three for four active. While you are carrying out one process you can be thinking ahead to the next move; while you smooth the way in the here and now, you can also ANTICIPATE far in advance. There are unlimited untapped resources hidden beneath the surface of our top level of consciousness. If, in the cool aftermath of a major blow-up, you spend a few moments analyzing the factors that brought it to a crisis, you may be able to make a plan for avoiding that same situation another time.

What Are Your Zero Hours?

Think about your "zero hours". We all have them...the time in the day when everything is just "too much". When my children were small and I was doubling as a breadwinner and parent, the hour between 5:00 and 6:00 was my Waterloo. It seemed as though my children always chose the time when I was trying to get dinner, to make demands. "I have to have $5.00 tomorrow!" or to blame me, "You forgot to put any dessert in my lunch today!", or to tattle on each other, "Bill had to go to the principal's office!" That was when they squabbled or teased each other until someone dissolved into tears. One day I called them together and made an announcement. "I am giving you fair warning," I stated, "I have had a rough day. I am tired and hungry and I am as cross as a bear. If you are smart you will find something to do and keep out of my way!" They looked at me with shocked surprise which turned to sympathy. It worked, at least that time! The eldest went down into the cellar to his workshop. The middle child, a girl, offered to play a game of Parcheesi with her younger brother. By the time we sat down to dinner, I was able to relax and smile again. I praised them for their cooperation and rewarded them with their favorite dessert. That was a case when *I* learned that it *makes sense to act in a certain way*.

Mrs. Fitzgerald, the young mother in our next story, found her zero hour at a different time. A single parent, working to support her four-year-old-son, she had no relatives or close friends nearby to call upon for help or guidance. Every Thursday (pay day), she took Michael with her to the supermarket while she shopped for the coming week. She needed to **ANTICIPATE**.

"Michael Fitzgerald, you put that back on the shelf and come right here!"

Vicki Stanton, the director of a day care center, was shopping for her family in the supermarket when she heard Mrs. Fitzgerald shrieking at her four-year-old-son. She had witnessed several scenes between this volatile little boy and his mother and she did not want to get drawn into this one, so she quickly moved an aisle away, but she could not help hearing the continuing hassle.

"Move when I call you or you'll get it when we go home," his mother shouted. Michael only grinned, carefully keeping out of reach. This was a favorite game — and he knew he could win. He glanced around, and seeing that he had an interested audience, he stuck his fingers in his ears and waved them at his mother, mocking her with a derisive "N'ya, N'ya, N'ya!"

The scenario continued until Michael's mother, finished

with her shopping, caught him and dragged him out the door screaming and crying. The last thing Vicki heard was Michael's angry shout, "You twisted my arm! Stop hurting me, you old fart!"

The following Monday a shamefaced mother sought the help of Michael's teacher.

"I saw you in the supermarket Thursday," she said. "I was so embarrassed! I hate to take Michael shopping with me but I have no one to leave him with. He just waits until we get where he knows everyone is looking at us, and then he starts to show off!"

"I saw that you were having a hard time," Vicki said quietly. "I'm sure many people were sympathizing with you but you probably felt that they were all criticizing you for being a bad mother!"

"Yes, that is exactly what I felt," this frustrated mother went on, relieved to find that someone understood. "Michael makes me feel so stupid...here I am, a grown woman, and that little rascal gets the better of me every time."

"Parenting isn't all fun and games," Vicki answered. "Children can be so sweet one minute—and drive us right up the wall a moment later."

"But maybe if I had more education I would know how to deal with Mike," Mrs. Fitzgerald went on. "You teachers never seem to have the problems we do."

"Oh yes, we do," Vicki replied, "but we have several advantages. If we have had a bad day, we can look forward to walking away from the situation. You can't! We want to do our best for your child but the real responsibility falls on your shoulders, and that is never-ending."

"Even more important, we have a support system which you are lacking. If Mike gives his teacher a hard time she can call on me, or one of the other teachers will step in and divert his attention.

"Also think about the environment here. Everything is planned to make life comfortable for children. Even the furniture is scaled down to their size. We can provide Mike with a place and program which fits his needs. When he goes with you into an adult world, he has to conform to a different set of standards.

"Now I suggest that before you to go the market again, you **ANTICIPATE**."

"Oh, I do," Mrs. Fitzgerald said with a wry grin, "and how I dread it!"

Vicki smiled and went on. "That wasn't exactly what I meant," she said. "As you **ANTICIPATE** the problem, look for ways to avoid it. You are tired and hungry when you pick up Michael on Thursday, but so is he. To you the shopping is a necessary chore. To Michael, it's a matter of trailing you around when he'd much rather be someplace else. He's not only tired and hungry, he's also bored. He wants your attention, and instead it's on the grocery list. It's not surprising that he acts up.

"Suppose you make Michael a partner. On Wednesday night, make out your list together. Give him some choices about which fruits or vegetables you are going to buy, and let him choose one kind of cookies or snacks. Then when you get to the store, let him find some of the items, matching labels and box fronts. We play all kinds of matching games at school — it's part of our reading readiness program — and Mike is very good at it. Just think how proud he would feel if he could demonstrate this to you in a useful way.

"Be sure to offer him the reward of praise when he does something helpful. For example:

"Michael, you were such a help to me, pushing the cart, carrying the bundles and putting the food away. After we eat, how about a story?"

"That makes a lot of sense," exclaimed Mrs. Fitzgerald. "And maybe Mike and I could go eat someplace *before* we shop. He'd love that."

"Good idea," agreed Vicki. "One thing more, though. All your problems aren't going to clear up in one fell swoop. Before you go out again, sit down and talk to Michael. Tell him how you feel when he misbehaves. Tell him what will happen if it occurs again, and be sure to follow through. Consistency is one of the most important keys to behavior management. It is part of the security children are seeking. Good luck, and let me know what happens."

We cannot foresee all of life's problems but when we know where the trouble spots are, we *can* learn to **ANTICIPATE** and plan ahead.

CHAPTER 3

Hesitate Before You Act

Joseph, an intelligent but emotionally high-strung, fourth-grader, stood facing his teacher with an angry, defiant expression. Their personalities were locked into a head-on collision! With a wild display of temper Joseph had destroyed a new game, thrown a chair across the room narrowly missing two other children, and shouted a string of obscenities at Mrs. Carruthers. It was the third such demonstration in one week, and she was at her wit's end. Her face was crimson with repressed anger — his, alternately taunting and frightened. "I need to buy a little time," she thought in desperation, "if I touch him I may hurt him — I am so angry!" Joseph, waiting for her to make the next move, was taken by surprise when she turned her back on him. Her twisting hands and white knuckles spoke of her feelings more loudly than words could have; even Joseph's youthful eyes couldn't fail to get the message. Finally, she turned around and in controlled tones said, "You know, Joseph, there are times when you make me so angry that I feel like YELLING at you," raising her voice to a shout. "Or I want to GRAB you and SHAKE YOU HARD," and she demonstrated with violent shaking movements but did not actually touch him. Joseph was awestruck. She had his full attention.

"But of course," she went on, "I can't do either of those things. I am a grown-up, and a teacher. I have to learn other ways to control my feelings! So I turned my back and took very deep breaths and counted to ten. You could see that it was hard — but if I hadn't done that I might have hurt you!

"The last time you had one of these awful temper tantrums, and we talked about it, you told me you could feel them coming on."

Joseph, thoroughly intrigued by now, and flattered to be the object of her attention, nodded in agreement.

"Yeah, it's like you said. It's like when the first rumblings of thunder warn us that a storm is coming."

"Well, you had to be intelligent to understand that," Mrs. Carruthers continued, "but you aren't being very smart when you fail to get the message! Your mind is supposed to tell your body what to do — but you are letting your body be the boss and tell your mind what to do. Instead of your *brain* making decisions, your arms and legs are in control — and they get you into trouble every time!

"Do you suppose my method could work for you? When you feel a temper tantrum coming on, could you take ten deep breaths? Like this...let's try it."

Together they took ten very deep breaths.

"There, that was good," Mrs. Carruthers said with an approving smile. "Now you see that if you could do that it would buy you some time — give your brain a chance to tell your body 'Hey, I'm in control here. I will be the boss! I will decide what you are going to do!'"

Joseph was still cautiously suspicious, but the idea of being the "boss" obviously intrigued him.

At this point, Mrs. Carruthers could almost see the wheels turning in Joseph's mind. She had given him a fascinating new idea — that he could be the BOSS of his own actions. It was obvious that his keen and absorbent mind was in high gear when he went back to his desk.

By **HESITATING**, Mrs. Carruthers accomplished two things. She gave herself time to cool her anger and approach Joseph in a calm and persuasive manner. She was also teaching Joseph, through her example and her specific suggestions, the value of stopping to think before acting.

When, in spite of your best efforts, you find yourself in the middle of a behavior problem, try to buy a little time. Turn your back! Walk away! Or just stand there looking intently and directly at the child. This lack of immediate action is often a surprise which takes a child off guard. It may change his train of thought from "I'll get her!" to "What is she going to do?", and in that few seconds you may change yours from, "Drat that kid!" He's doing it to me again!" to "What can be going on within this child that makes him feel so mean?"

CHAPTER 4

Investigate the Cause

Mrs. Carruthers did not stop with the suggestions she planted in Joseph's mind. She moved on with the third step in my plan—**INVESTIGATE**.

Seeking Clues to Behavior

First, she checked into Joseph's family situation. In a conference with his mother she discovered that his father had died when he was two years old, and that since then he had been the only "man" in the house. Recently his mother had remarried. He was no longer the king pin and the power he had always been able to exert over his mother with temper tantrums and sulking was no longer effective. To make matters worse, his new stepfather brought two sons with him...both older and stronger than Joseph. They had been given his room, and he had been required to move into a much smaller one. It was plain to see that this child was hurting and knowing this helped his teacher to understand some of his behavior. Small wonder that the notion of "being the boss" had been attractive!

In the child care center, when the behavior of a child becomes a constant source of irritation, a wise caregiver could ask her director or supervisor to help her look for clues in the following areas:

PEOPLE

ENVIRONMENT

PROGRAM

First, she can go to the office to see what is recorded about this child. The application form will contain information about his family. Does he have two parents? Do they both work? Has he any brothers or sisters? Is he the youngest, the eldest, or a middle child? Has he recently been displaced by a new baby?

If that information is not enough, the director may ask additional questions such as "Has there been a major shake-up in the family recently? Is some close family member seriously ill? Has there been a recent death of a beloved relative — or of a pet? Has the child been involved in or witnessed an accident? Has the family moved recently?" These are sensitive questions and the inquirer must tread lightly — ready to back off at the slightest sign of resentment. It is a task for the director — not the classroom caregiver.

The director can also talk to the various individuals who may observe or care for this child in the course of a day. If she encounters conflicting opinions; if one person finds him an interesting, intelligent child, and another describes him as a "fresh, smart-talking brat," she may have put her finger on a sore spot.

Next, in her search for evidence, the caregiver may look at the *environment*. The standards we set for children's behavior must be based on what we know of their developmental needs. When our expectations are contrary to their natural instincts, something has to give. In the child care center we may have become so "accustomed to the place" that we fail to see where we have created a problem. For example, if the furnishings are so arranged that there are long corridors, we waste our energy if we constantly admonish "No running!" A simple solution is to set up some dividers to break up that space and remove the temptation.

Sometimes it helps to invite an outsider to observe in the center, paying particular attention to the environment. Or it can be made the subject of a staff meeting. I personally recall one such meeting where the pre-announced topic was Discipline. Each participant was asked to describe a particular child who was giving her trouble, and the rest of the group offered suggestions.

"I have a wild bunch of four-year-olds," one teacher stated. "They are noisy and rough and destructive."

"Could it be something in the environment?" one of her colleagues asked.

A barrage of questions followed:

"Do you have enough equipment to keep everyone occupied?"

"Is it easily accessible?"

"Do you have an orderly system so children put things back when they have finished with them?"

"Do you give children tools that work?"

"Do the scissors really cut?"

"Is the hammer heavy enough to pound a nail?"

"We talk about encouraging children to have good ideas and to be creative, but don't we sometimes frustrate them because we don't give them the proper tools?"

That's right, we do," another put in. "But my pet peeve is the housekeeping corner. It is the most popular place in the whole center and sometimes I shudder at what we are teaching the children who play in it. Dress-up clothes all jumbled in a carton! We don't throw dresses, shoes, hats and pocketbooks all together in our homes! And dirty! It only takes a little extra effort to keep the doll clothes and the blankets on the doll bed clean—and the children love to help wash them. It's the first place I look when I visit a center—if it makes me wish I were little again so I could play in it, I give it an A plus!"

"Right—and it needs to change often—to enrich the kind of play that goes on," was another comment. "A suitcase or brief case—a hair dryer—just adding one thing—starts a whole new trend of activity."

"When you are checking the environment, don't forget to look for soft, quiet places where a child can be alone," was the last comment.

It was safe to assume that each one of those teachers went back to look at her *own* center with a critical eye, and that they

may have found the answers to their problems of discipline in the environment.

The problem-solving teacher next turns to *program*. Sometimes we impose rigid routines—for no better reason than because "we have always done it that way." Each day is just like the one before. Play must end promptly at ten o'clock because it is time for juice. We drag children away from an activity in which they may have been thoroughly engrossed—without asking ourselves if it makes sense.

I was visiting in a center when the teacher brought forth a new manipulative game—a set of interlocking plastic frames. Four little girls sat down at a table and played with them contentedly. One by one, three of them drifted away to play elsewhere, but Jessie was completely absorbed. Her involvement was so intense that she did not even look up when the teacher announced it was time for juice. At the end of an hour, she rose with a sigh of satisfaction, carefully put the pieces back in the box, placed the box on the shelf, and joined the other children who were now listening to a story. I was impressed with the wisdom and understanding of that teacher who let Jessie stay with her new interest.

Marveling at her staying power, I asked, "Does she always get so involved with that type of activity?"

"Quite the contrary," was the reply. "She normally spends most of her time in dramatic play—and she seldom stays with anything for more than fifteen minutes. This was a side of Jessie we have never seen before—which is why I couldn't think of disturbing her! It would have been a shame to break in on that marvelous concentration!"

Can these same methods apply in the home? Can a parent who is struggling with a particular problem of behavior seek answers by looking at the *people, environment* and her daily schedule or *program*? I believe that the answer is yes.

"Who has time to think about all that stuff?" the harried mother might exclaim, but if she were to add up the minutes in a day which she spends in yelling, scolding, repeating admonitions, arguing, reasoning, and spanking, she might find that the time is there and could be used more profitably.

Recently I met with a small group of young mothers who wanted to talk about discipline. The problems they described were the usual ones. "My little girl bites me. It hurts. What shall I do? Should I bite her back?"

"My three-year-old is driving me mad. He persists in jumping off the back of the big chair in the living room."

"I can't make my two-year-old stop pulling the lamp cord out at the base plugs. I have scolded and spanked—and he still goes right on. All the time I am telling him not to touch he looks me right in the eye and does it again."

As we discussed the three points to **INVESTIGATE**— *people, environment* and *program*, each of these mothers began to see that there was more than one way to look for solutions.

The first mother may have had a *people* problem. She was advised to note what happened just prior to each biting incident to see whether there was a consistent pattern. Was it when another adult came into the picture, either in person or on the phone? Was her child asking for more attention? Rebelling against correction?

It was plain to see that the lively three-year-old-boy was just "doing what comes naturally" at that age. Using chairs or a table tipped over, card-table with a blanket thrown over it, a step stool, some pillows and cardboard cartons, his mother could create an obstacle course which would give him legitimate opportunities to crawl through, climb over and under, and jump off. It was also suggested that a door gym, which can be hung from the door frame, and which can be converted to a swing, a trapeze bar, rings and a climbing rope would help satisfy his need.

The simplest solution for the third mother was to unplug the lamp during the day and to keep his prying fingers out of the plugs with protective covers. In her anxiety to be a good mother she felt that giving in to him would create problems later. She saw it as her duty to "make him mind." She was also urged to be prepared with diversionary tactics, to be ready with interesting alternatives when she came smack up against this child's will.

And so **INVESTIGATE** is the third step in our plan. When all is said and done, when rules are made, and a plan is in operation, it then becomes necessary to **COMMUNICATE**.

CHAPTER 5

Communicate — Open the Doors of Understanding

The simplest, most readily available tool we have in dealing with our children is the ability to **COMMUNICATE** with spoken words, rather than physical force. Language is the oil which lubricates the journey through life. Words enable us to make our feelings known, to ask for what we need, to explain what we mean, to pass on information, and to offer support and encouragement to others. On the negative side words can act as weapons. They can inflict emotional damage more lasting than a physical blow, and they can arouse confusion in the young child's mind as was demonstrated by Aaron, aged three.

He was found by his mother on the front lawn of his home, waving his arms up and down, crying bitterly.

"Whatever is the matter?" his anxious mother inquired.

"You and Daddy are going to Miami to visit grandmother — and I can't go!" he said, between sobs.

"But of course you are going with us!" his mother reassured him. "I think if we showed up without you, grandmother would send us right back!"

"But you said we are going to fly — and I haven't learned to fly yet!" was the tearful response.

The development of language in the young child is one of life's marvels we take for granted. Between the time he speaks that first word and the age of five the average child will have acquired a large part of his basic vocabulary. His comprehension

NO! NO! NO!

may take longer, as Aaron's predicament made clear. The sensitive teacher or parent will be tuned in to the second language, behavior, which is often a child's only way of letting us know what he is feeling. Words for basic needs, "I want some milk," "Help me to put on my jacket," are learned easily. Words which say, "I'm scared," "I'm confused," "I'm angry." "I'm jealous!" are hard for even grown-ups to express.

Oral communication is a skill. One which can be taught, and which improves with practice. Even the tiny infant is absorbing words, storing them away on the film in his brain where they can be resurrected later and put to use. In our infant centers, we instruct our staff to talk to the babies, explaining what they are doing. "I am going to wash you and put on a nice clean diaper;" or naming objects, "This is a basket. It is filled with crackers." Even though one would have to question the degree of comprehension, this is what is called in computer language "input," and when the programming is constant and consistent, the "output" will emerge at such an early age as to be astounding.

Language brings a sense of power to the toddler who discovers that the word "No" elicits a reaction. He uses it indiscriminately, often with little idea of its meaning, and the adult who tries to "make something of it" will be the loser; not necessarily at that moment, but in future relationships. To make issues over prompt obedience at this stage is like trying to drive a car when the steering mechanism is broken — it can't function without the proper equipment! Marge, a teacher who *expected* the children to do what she wanted them to, was a master at dealing with these little ones. "Oh yes, we will!" she would say with a smile, and taking the child by the hand, would proceed to follow through on her request. Recognizing his need to assert his independence she wouldn't have dreamed of engaging in a confrontation with a child; this is in sharp contrast to a young father I witnessed recently who shouted, "No two year old is going to tell me!!!!"

There does come a time (usually at about age three) when comprehension sets in. The child understands the meaning of "no" but continues to test the limits of his power to resist. The burden is then on the adult to substitute positive statements for negative directions. "Walk in back of the swings" or "Come this way" instead of "I told you not to run in front of the swings!" "Take another bite of your dinner" instead of "Stop messing around and clean up your plate!"

Many adults fail to realize how much their children can understand if given the chance. They talk *about* them, and *in front* of them, but not *to* them.

Pouring Fuel on the Flames

"Good morning, Tony," said the teacher with a warm smile, as the handsome, blonde, four-year-old came into the nursery school. Instead of the cheerful response she expected, Tony brushed past her and went directly to the cubby area. In a moment there was a shriek of outrage.

"Tony knocked my coat down and put his jacket on my hook!"

"Why, Tony," exclaimed Sue in surprise. "Why did you do that? You know which is your cubby. Here's your own picture on it."

The only answer was a defiant glare. For the next hour Tony moved through the classroom like a tornado, leaving anger and destruction in his wake.

"Tony scribbled on my picture!"

"Miss Davis, make Tony get out of here! He knocked down our airport!"

"Tony hit me!"

"Tony took my baseball cap that my daddy gave me!"

With each episode, Sue's patience grew thinner, her exasperation stronger, and her reprimands sharper. The last straw came when she saw Tony grab one corner of the cloth on a small table, sending the carefully-laid tea party to the floor.

"Tony, this is too much! I can't think what has gotten into you today. You're usually such a good boy, but you have been naughty all morning. How can you expect to have any friends when you are so mean to them? Now you will have to come into my office and sit on a chair until you can behave."

Tony stared at her defiantly and did not budge. Rather than drag him, Sue picked up the rigid, resistant child and carried him into her office, where she sat him down, none too gently.

"I can't imagine what's wrong with you today, Tony," she said again. "I think I'll have to call your mother."

As if her words had opened a valve, the child burst into wild sobbing, and his rigid body crumpled.

Sue's anger dissolved as she looked at him. "Oh, Tony," she said softly. "What is it, sweetheart? What has happened?" She picked him up gently, sat down in a big chair and held him close, making small, comforting sounds until his sobbing diminished. Again she asked, "What's wrong, Tony?"

He buried his head in her shoulder, and in muffled tones he said, "They took my mother away. She was all white. She had her eyes shut. They took her away in a big van with a siren."

"It's all right, dear. Everything is going to be all right," she said soothingly, as her mind raced with speculation. What had happened at Tony's house, and why in the world hadn't someone told her about it? And why, she thought, didn't I do some **INVESTIGATING** when he acted so unlike himself?

What *had* happened at Tony's house that morning? Tony's mother, three months pregnant, was awakened by sharp pains and found that she was bleeding profusely. Steve, her husband, called the doctor, who ordered an ambulance to get her to the hospital. Frantic with fear for his wife, Steve just barely had enough presence of mind to call his neighbor, Mrs. Anderson, and ask her to take care of Tony.

Tony came out into the hall in his pajamas in time to see two men carrying a thing that looked like a bed. His mother was on it, very white, eyes closed. The men carried her down the stairs and out the front door. Tony began to tremble. Just then his father dashed out of his room, putting on his jacket as he came.

"Daddy," cried Tony. "Where are they taking Mummy?"

Barely pausing, his father answered quickly, "Mommy's sick. Mrs. Anderson will help you get dressed and get you ready for school. Be a good boy." As he rushed off, Tony ran to the window. The two men were closing the doors of a big van like Uncle Harry's, except that this one had a flashing light on the roof, and as it drove off a siren began to wail. Tony's stomach started churning, and he thought he was going to throw up.

Just then Mrs. Anderson came in and went into his room, pulling out drawers and looking for clothes. Hurriedly she dressed him, brushing aside his anxious questions. She hustled him across the street to her house, and gave him some breakfast, but he couldn't eat. His mind was whirling with questions. Where were they taking his mother? Why didn't Daddy take him, too? Why did his mother look so funny? Who were those men? Why was Mummy sick? What did that mean? Sick meant staying in bed and swallowing medicine, not being carried away, all white and still. Was she ever coming back?

He tried to ask Mrs. Anderson, but she kept saying, "I don't know. Hurry up, the school bus will be here any minute." Just then the driver of the nursery school station wagon tooted, and Mrs. Anderson rushed him out the door. She didn't kiss him goodbye, the way his mother always did.

Tony's small world had suddenly turned topsy-turvy, and he was scared. All the way to school he was quiet, not chattering with his friends. But as he went, his fear spilled over into anger, which exploded into action as soon as he went in the door.

There is a message in this story for both teachers and parents. Sue Davis failed to apply two of the key steps in dealing with a child who is misbehaving, **HESITATE** and **INVESTI-GATE.** Tony's behavior was contrary to his usual pattern, which should have caused her to **HESITATE.** If she had practiced the policy of "getting into the skin of the child" she would have said to herself, "Something must have happened to set off this unusual behavior. Until I get some clues, I will move with caution." Instead she reacted with anger and disapproval, thus pouring additional fuel on flames that were already burning in this troubled little boy.

As for **INVESTIGATING,** her first move should have been to call his home. In this case, since there was no one to answer, she would have turned to the emergency number listed, which might have been Mrs. Anderson's.

Most of all, this story points up the need to **COMMUNI-CATE.** If Tony's grandmother had been living in the house, would Tony's father have brushed *her* aside so brusquely? No, he would have taken the minute or two necessary to explain what was happening. With the ambulance there and his wife on the way to the help she needed, Steve should have taken time to ease Tony's mind. "Mommy is sick, and those men are taking her to the hospital where the doctor will take care of her. She's going to be all right, and in a few days she will be home. I can't take you with me because they don't let little boys in the hospital unless they are sick, but I will be here when you come home from school."

Likewise, in turning Tony over to Mrs. Anderson, he should have quickly briefed her on what had happened, and asked her to explain to the driver of the station wagon, who, in turn, would have alerted the teacher.

Adults do not always think of the viewpoint of the child who has only existed on this earth for 36 to 48 months. We take their comprehension for granted. In any crisis, it is important to be sensitive to the concerns aroused in the child, and to explain the things that might be beyond his realm of experience. If this is not done, confusion and anger will manifest themselves in the only way he knows how to COMMUNICATE—through his behavior. How much less painful this whole situation would have been for Tony if the lines of communication had been open!

Communicating with adults is often difficult for young children because they have discovered that grown-ups can't be trusted. They are often punished for telling the truth, or explaining their feelings. Unfortunately, parents who test their children's love are not as uncommon as we might like to believe! An extreme example of the way a foolish parent destroyed her child's ability to trust follows.

CHAPTER **6**

Basic Trust

With a strange, choking sound Mary Alice dropped to the floor and appeared to be unconscious.

"Mama! Mama!" screamed Audrey, her six-year-old daughter. "Are you sick? What is the matter? Please talk to me," she cried, patting her mother's cheek. "Oh, what shall I do?"

After what seemed an eternity to Audrey, her mother sat up, laughing, and said, "I'm all right. I just wanted to see how much you love me!"

As she related this story Audrey, now thirty years old and a mother herself, shuddered at the memory. "My mother was young and pretty," she said. "She loved it when people said we looked more like sisters than mother and daughter. But I didn't want to be her sister. She was my mother and I wanted her to be like the other kid's mothers. Everyone thought she was such a *good* mother. She kept my hair curled and dressed me in frilly dresses. I was really more like her doll than her child—and she treated me with the same inconsistency. One minute she was hugging and kissing me—and the next she turned away and ignored me. There were times she wouldn't speak to me for days and I never knew what I had done to offend her, but I was miserable because I was sure it had to be something bad. I carried a constant burden of guilt. It wasn't until I ended up on a psychiatrist's couch years later that I realized what she had done to me with her childish tricks. I couldn't trust anyone—the husband I loved, or my own children. That lack of trust has affected my whole life. I was always sure that someone was cheating me; the garage man had put someone else's worn out tire on my car; the gas station attendant charged me the wrong price; the storekeeper had his thumb on the scales. The only way I can bear to maintain a relationship with my mother now is to try to feel sorry for her," Audrey continued sadly. "She is still wrapped up in herself and I'm sure she has no idea what she did to me!"

Trust is the Core of Relationships

Basic trust begins at the moment of birth when the infant emerges from the protected warm environment of the womb into a cold, harsh world where his senses are assaulted with light and noise. If he is treated with loving care, fed when he is hungry, changed when he is wet and uncomfortable, cuddled and comforted, he comes to know the world as a good place, and his beginning self-concept is founded on security and trust.

But what if he is neglected? Fed only after he cries himself purple? Left sodden in his crib for hours? What if his most important needs for touching and being touched are ignored? What will his impressions of the world be then?

The seeds of insecurity which Mary Alice planted in her little daughter's developing "self" grew into an ugly weed of distrust, which affected her relationships with people throughout her life.

Parents Are Not Always Perfect

However, there is such a thing as letting the pendulum swing too far the other way. Parents' feelings are important too. In your efforts to do what is best for your child, there will be failures. You must not let yourself be eaten up with guilt if you lose your temper or if you say the wrong thing or in any way betray your own goals. We aren't perfect. We do the best we can.

In Audrey's case, her ability to cope with her mother's foolishness was hampered by the image presented to the outside world of a loving, caring relationship. Each time she heard her mother receive compliments for being such a *good* mother it reinforced her belief that she must be a *bad* child!

Child Abuse Isn't Always Physical

The immature behavior exhibited by Mary Alice in this story leaves us with feelings of shock and disgust. This was a clear case of abuse, but because there were no visible signs of physical harm, it went undetected. Child abuse has been brought out into the public view in recent years and legislation requiring an observer to report it or be subject to a fine is a step in the right direction. The kind of emotional abuse Mary Alice inflicted on Audrey is more subtle, and less likely to be observed than black and blue marks and cigarette burns; but the ill effects are just as serious, and may even be more lasting.

How then do we instill a feeling of trust in our children? The first key is love—steady, unqualified, undemanding **LOVE.** Love which allows liberty but will not tolerate license; love which offers security and protection but is able to let go when the fledgling is ready to fly. A parent may say "I do not like that thing you are doing—but I will never stop loving you."

The second element is **RESPECT.** Some parents treat their children as if they were toys—inanimate objects put on this earth for their amusement or to do their bidding. They talk about their good and bad features in their presence, acting as if they were not persons who can hear. They embarrass and humiliate them before others, criticizing their appearance, behavior, or attempts to be like adults.

"Go wash that filthy face!" Mother says to Sally as she comes running in from her play to greet her visiting grandmother. "Nana doesn't want to kiss a dirty face!"

"You've put your pants on backwards," Father says to Jackie. "How stupid can you get? Go right back into your room and change them!" when he might better have ignored the mistake and congratulated his son for dressing himself.

And parents aren't the only ones guilty of such rude behavior.

"Not very **P-R-E-T-T-Y,**" one visitor spelled out to another. "No, but very **S-M-A-R-T!**" five-year-old Deborah interjected, with a gleeful look in her eye.

There is a simple basic rule which, if followed by parents, would prevent a lot of problems.

Treat your children with the same courtesy you would accord a guest in your home!

And so we build our trust relationship on **LOVE** and **RESPECT;** the third ingredient is **CONSISTENCY.** The parent who is indulgent and amused by a particular bit of behavior one day, but reacts with screaming and punishment when the pattern is repeated on another occasion leaves the child in a state of confusion. He *wants* to please the adult who holds the key to his security; he *needs* to feel the approval of that person, but how can he know what will win it for him when the rules change every day?

It is hard to be consistent. Adults who have problems with discipline may never have faced up to their own feelings. They are afraid to admit to their own hostility, and since punishment is, at least in their view, an act of aggression, they are unable to take a firm stand. Furthermore, adults themselves are subject to mood changes. When everything is going smoothly it is easy to be patient, reasonable and understanding, but in the pressurized world we confront today that state of euphoria seldom exists for long. The working mother who comes home at the end of a stressful day and is greeted by a whining, fretful child has to dig deep in her well of inner reserves to behave with consistency, love and respect.

What is the key to this all-important consistency? How does a parent go about achieving it?

Set the ground rules. In your own mind, decide what standards of behavior are important, and how you can enforce them.

For example, if you do not want your children to "talk back," or give saucy replies to adults, make up your mind that you will *never* laugh at such behavior or treat it lightly.

In a two-parent family, guidelines for behavior must be established and agreed upon in advance. When this harmony is lacking a bright child will quickly grasp the opportunity to "play" one parent against the other.

CHAPTER 7

Doing What
Comes Naturally

Up to this point we have been talking about disciplinary situations which had dramatic beginnings, when in fact most of our troubles revolve around the simple, necessary routines of daily living. Eating, eliminating, and sleeping are natural processes. Nature has seen to it that they will happen without our interference.

It is so easy to let these routine procedures develop into headlock confrontations.

"What will 'they' think of me if my child isn't toilet trained," the frustrated mother agonizes.

"I'm supposed to give my child a nutritionally balanced diet — but no one tells me what to do when he won't even taste vegetables!"

Caregivers in a child care center have some of the same anxieties, but for different reasons. "They," at least in their imagination, can be critical of their performance as teachers — but "they" may also hold the key to job security and professional advancement.

Instead of building simple, necessary practices into "deadlocks" we might well listen to the advice of an experienced teacher in a day care center.

"Louise," one of the younger caregivers said, "how does it happen that when you eat with the children everyone is so quiet and peaceful? They never throw the food around or leave a big mess under the table."

"Yes, and I don't hear the kids at your table saying 'Yuk! I hate this stuff,' the way some of mine do" another teacher chimed in. It only takes one, and my whole group decides not to eat. I think Sammy Green just does it to get my goat!"

"And how is it that when you are in charge of the nap room everyone goes to sleep?" another beginning teacher inquired. "When I know my turn is coming up, I start dreading it as soon as I wake up in the morning! They just seem to be waiting for me! No one sleeps! One starts jumping on his cot and then another and the more I scold the worse they get! Just when I think I have them all settled down someone has to go to the bathroom and that starts another round! By the time they all settle down — *if* they do — I am the one who needs the nap!"

Louise, a woman in her fifties with an ample bosom and a readily available lap, looked up in surprise. "Well," she answered slowly and thoughtfully, "I guess they just know I like them — and they want to please me. I sort of *expect* that they will do what I ask them to — and they do it!"

It sounded much too simple, but Louise was right. Young children are quick to sense it when an adult is apprehensive. When they discover that negative behavior can arouse anxiety in a teacher they make the most of it. But actually, down deep, most children do not really want it that way. It makes them uneasy when an adult abdicates from the position of authority. They need to be able to press against the security of boundaries, and know that they will remain firm. "I know my mother (teacher) will not let me" feels better than a shaky, "Who will stop me if I go too far?"

Eating

Trouble in the home often starts with an over-anxious mother.

"Eat your vegetables!" she says. "They are good for you!" and when Jimmy says, "NO, I hate vegetables!" she lets a simple situation build up into a battle of wills.

"I'm not going to eat that icky stuff," Hilary whines, pushing back her plate petulantly. "You know I hate spaghetti! Why did you give it to me?"

Instead of a calm, "That is what we are having today. If you don't want to eat it, you can have bread and peanut butter," Mother caters to this child's whim.

"How would you like a nice poached egg on toast?" she offers, and lets her own meal get cold while she hurries to prepare it.

"Clean up everything on that plate or you can't have any dessert," Father thunders.

"If you don't at least taste the broccoli, there will be no television for you tonight!" Mother warns.

Eating should be taken for granted. Threats, bribes and rewards attach undue importance to an act which should be as matter-of-fact as breathing. If you throw down the gauntlet by issuing a threat, you must expect your bright, intelligent child to accept the challenge. Suddenly you find yourself in a confrontation of your own creating: a situation in which some-one will have to back down, unless, of course, you take advantage of your superior strength and resort to punishment.

Does any of this strike a familiar note? If you have been trapped into a battle of wills over eating, how can you extricate yourself?

First, stop worrying. A normal, healthy child will not starve if he misses a meal. In fact, when the attention ceases to focus on him he will probably eat what you put before him. He may not eat as much as you think he should, and he may not choose to eat it in the order you suggest, but he *will* eat when he is hungry.

A Touch of Class

The second bit of advice is to create an environment which is conducive to gracious living if you want your child to acquire social skills. When my children were young, I discovered that when we ate in the kitchen I was continually nagging.

"Stop tipping your chair back! You are digging holes in the linoleum!"

"Ask your sister to pass the butter — you don't have to reach across the table."

"Don't try to talk with your mouth full!"

But when we ate in the dining room by candlelight and on the best dishes, my offspring rose to the occasion! An attractive setting seemed to lead automatically to better manners and good conversation. It even worked on me! I tended to give more thought to the way I prepared and served the food. That is probably when I learned what I so often preach, "If you treat your children with the same courtesy that you accord a guest in your home, many of your behavioral conflicts will just melt away." We all like to be proud of our children when we take them out to eat — either in a restaurant or in a friend's home. Somewhere they have to learn the skills — and home should be the training ground!

When I talk with my grown-up children about what they remember of their early years, they will often say "The times we sat around the table after dinner, just talking." It was a time for sharing, for easy conversation. When I was a child, the adults talked and the children waited until they were invited to speak. Years later, when I was a student at Tufts I listened with a tinge of envy when a young woman explained how she had learned to take such concise notes.

"You must have had an excellent English teacher in high school," I commented. "No," she said. "It was my father who taught us how to extract the meat from a lecture or story. Each Sunday we were required to come to the table prepared to talk about something we had read in that day's paper. With skillful questioning and without causing us embarrassment he helped us to see what was truly important."

"Did you feel it was a chore?" I asked. "Didn't you resent it?"

"Not really," she replied. "In the first place it was an accepted practice. I guess it didn't occur to me that this wasn't going on in other homes! But it was also interesting. I didn't know I was being taught something which would mean so much later!"

I'll admit that this example is idealistic, and is not likely to happen in the average home but there can be some rules established which will make mealtime pleasurable. It should be agreed that squabbling and arguing cannot be tolerated at the table. Dinner time should never be used to play back the day's mistakes and misdemeanors. Subjects which stir the emotions, and interfere with digestion, such as Jim's report card, whether Kathy is going out after dinner, or why Hank can't use the family car, should be reserved for a more appropriate time and place. It is pretty hard to enjoy food when your stomach is knotted with anxiety or resentment!

Table Manners

"But if I don't call attention to table manners how can I expect my children to learn?" an anxious parent queries.

"By setting a good example," is the answer. "Imagine that you are sitting at a banquet. If a fellow guest slurps his soup, or eats his peas with his knife you do not criticize him in front of the other guests! Your children are entitled to the same consideration. Mention an error later, in a casual way, when you are alone. Praise him quietly when you see that he has made a conscious effort to improve!"

Mealtime in the Child Care Center

The main responsibility for the upbringing of the child rests with the parents but the reality of the times is that more than half of our children are spending eight to ten hours in child care outside the home while the mother is working. This means that it is the caregiver who is providing a role model. When I was seeking material for a book on Day Care, I visited more than 150 centers in 22 states. One of the criteria I had chosen for determining quality care was the manner in which the meal was conducted. I was looking for programs which made a real effort to duplicate the environment of a good home. In some of the worst places, I saw teachers standing around eating off their plates, chatting with each other while they kept a desultory eye on their charges who were seated at tables. The children in some cases were silent, others were noisy, grabbing, standing up to get what they wanted without waiting to have food passed. The teachers either ignored them or barked sharp admonitions. It was *not* a model of good eating!

In the best center I saw children helping to set the table. One child was chosen to go to the kitchen for the food. One adult sat at each table and served the food. (The director explained that when two adults were at a table, they were inclined to talk to each other, excluding the children. One of the goals at mealtime was to encourage conversation, with every child participating.)

A set of rules had been drawn up with the help of the children, and posted on the wall near the table. Thus the teacher could say "Look at number 7, Jackie," instead of "How many times do I have to tell you not to stuff so much into your mouth at one time!"

The teacher made one thing clear at the outset. "If you do not like what we are having to eat you will not talk about it. You may think about it, but we do not wish to hear it. Tell us if something looks or tastes good — or better still, tell Mrs. Jones (the cook). It will make her happy."

You Can't Win!

To conclude the subject of eating, there is one thought that seldom occurs to the adult. In most of life's situations the child is at your mercy, he must conform because you are bigger and stronger. When it comes to eating he holds the trump card. You may be able to force a child to eat, you can hold his nose so he has to swallow, but you *cannot* make him retain it. Push him too far and he will manage to bring it back up!

Eliminating

This same principle applies to toilet training, another area in which the child holds the power. I get a desperate letter every so often from some poor teacher or director who pleads, "What can we do with the four-year-old who messes his pants day after day? We make him sit on the toilet until he has ridges on his bottom with no results, and then he will deliberately soil himself. Why would an apparently normal child do this?"

Toddlers will have accidents — and two's and three's may occasionally be too preoccupied with playing or wait too long before going to the toilet, but when a child of four or older has innumerable accidents it is time to **INVESTIGATE**. The parents, teachers and someone with professional training need to work as a team to discover the underlying cause. Occasionally the problem is reversed; a child will withhold his bowel movements. The cause may be physical or psychological but in either case it is a warning of a problem which should not be ignored.

Sleeping

The third function which nature provided for is sleeping, and again this often becomes the battleground for clashing wills. The key is consistency. Again, I think it helps to state the rules on paper, leaving no ground for argument. A sample might be: Bedtime is seven thirty.

At seven o'clock

1. get undressed
2. go to the bathroom
3. wash hands
4. brush teeth
5. say goodnight to the family
6. get into bed where you may:
        have a story read to you,
        or listen to one record, or
        look at books.

At seven thirty the light will be put out.

To avoid the issue of "one more drink of water" place a glass of water or milk on the table beside the child's bed. Do *not* respond to conversation once she is in bed. It can go on for as long as you are willing to prolong it!

There will be arguments: "Why should I have to go to bed at seven-thirty if Danny can stay up until eight?"

"I had a long nap at school today. I'm not tired!"

"If I promise to go to bed very fast, can I stay up just this once to watch this program?"

Sometimes the problem isn't just in getting the child to bed but in keeping him there. It may start when he is frightened by a nightmare or a sudden storm. He awakens a sleepy mother who takes the easy way out and lets him crawl in beside her. It's cozy and warm, much nicer than being in a separate room all alone; and one can hardly blame him for repeating the visit. Hard as it is at the time to get out of bed and put him back in his own bed, staying a while if necessary to comfort him, the end result will be best for all concerned.

Some children get out of bed and wander through the house while their parents are sleeping — a dangerous habit. There is no easy solution. I *cannot* condone locking the child in — I *would* offer as many compromises as you can stand, such as "You may turn on your light and play as long as you stay in your own room and are quiet."

Buy a lunchbox and pack a little snack; he may be really hungry.

Tape a story and let him listen to your voice. (End it with "Now turn out your light and go to sleep.")

Adults should use a reasonable degree of understanding of special situations or circumstances, but variations ought to be rare. If rules change frequently they lose significance — it then becomes a matter of who can win the debate!

Children need to know that it is the adult who makes the decisions. I have seen parents let their children rationalize, argue, explain and reason ad infinitum, when they should have said, "This is the way it is — with no better reason than, "Because I say so!"

These three functions: eating, sleeping, and eliminating are necessary for survival. Society imposes additional skills which can bring on another whole set of behavior problems. Children have to learn to clothe their bodies and keep them clean. We live in such a hurried, busy world that parents, at least, are tempted to do for the child what he can really learn to do for himself.

Dressing

"Here, let me do it!" mother says in an exasperated tone as she tugs on boots. "I haven't got all day to wait for you!"

"No, I can't wait for you to get dressed. I'll be late for work!" as she hustles her daughter into her clothes.

In the nursery school or day care center, there should always be TIME. Teachers can slowly and patiently teach children the HOW, and give them ample time to do it themselves. Learning to button, zip, tie and lace are part of the education process, and the child's "I AM" grows with each small success.

The reverse problem is occasionally one of getting a child to keep his clothes on. A teacher in a child care center related an amusing situation. Jackie insisted on taking his shoes off and walking around the classroom in his bare feet. His teacher had tried being patient, stern, cross, and punishing with no success. One day Jackie came to her.

"I'll make you a proposition!" he said.

Wondering where a four-year-old might have heard those words, she answered, "O.K. What is it?"

"I'll keep my shoes on if you will let me move the sink (in the housekeeping area)."

"Sure, where do you want to put it?" she queried.

"Over here, so I can look out the window when I wash the dishes," was the answer. And holding true to his word, he did keep his shoes on after that!

Teaching a child how to wash his hands and face carefully and dry them, how to brush his teeth and take care of his toileting procedures are all a legitimate part of the pre-school program. Remembering their own schooling, caregivers are inclined to think "curriculum" relates only to intellectual activities, when actually skills for daily living are the foundation which makes later learning possible.

Going back to parents, there is one thing they can do which will save wear and tear on them and encourage the child. They can look at the *environment*— and the way it prevents children from doing the very things we demand of them. The mother who sends her child back to wash his face again might have saved that irritation if she had placed a mirror over the washstand at his eye level.

When a full length mirror is easily accessible a child can be taught to take a last look— and possibly discover that his socks don't match or his shirt has a big dirty smudge.

Home environments are designed for adults with little or no consideration for the difficulties they present for children. If each of us had to spend one whole day in a house which was built for giants with tables, chairs, beds and toilets which were proportionally as outsized as the furniture we expect our children to use, we might be more understanding of their problems. We can put a small stool in the bathroom, which can be used in front of the toilet and washbowl. We can hang a towel rack where little hands can reach it. Going back to the analogy of the guest, we know that a considerate hostess anticipates the needs of overnight guests and tries to make them comfortable. Can we do less for our children?

A Sense of Order

Before we leave the subject of *environment,* let's take a look at the demands we make on children to maintain a neat appearance—and keep their belongings in order. How much help do we give them? One facet of Montessori training with which I wholeheartedly agree is the emphasis on a child's need for order. From his earliest days if there is a "place for everything" and he is expected to put things back in that place when he is finished with them, a basic training process is set in motion which will pay dividends in every step of learning. Ordering objects is a foundation for reading and math. Ordering thought processes is essential to formal education. It begins with the ability to *see the sense* in putting things where they belong.

It is ideal if each child can have a closet for his clothing with hooks at eye level and a clothes rod which moves up gradually as he grows, but surely the poorest home can have nails on the wall.

It is nice if children can learn to pile their underwear, socks

and jerseys neatly in bureau drawers; but three shoe boxes, decorated and marked, can serve the same purpose.

Speaking of boxes and order, I can't miss an opportunity to speak of my pet peeve—the traditional toy chest. It may be very attractive on the outside, but it teaches all the wrong things. When mother stands at the door of a room and says, "Clean up this mess immediately!" what does the child do? Scoops everything up and throws it into the box. When he slams the lid down the room may look better, but how can we berate him for being destructive when we teach him to throw small cars, puzzle pieces, coloring books, broken crayons and torn books all into one magnificent glory hole!!! The toy chest is the ultimate example of adult stupidity and inconsistency!

How do you replace it? Provide low shelves (boards on cement blocks will do). Draw pictures to fit each object to show where it belongs. Again the shoe boxes (which most stores are glad to provide free) can be utilized to store the small toys. In a good child care center the children are taught how to take care of the property. When they are allowed to be careless with their own things at home we teach them the wrong lessons in the same way that Zelda taught her son "to hit people."

CHAPTER 8

Behavior That Bugs You

The problems discussed in the previous chapter are all the results of over-zealous attempts to "train" children to do what should come "naturally". We often act like the gardener who can't wait for nature to produce the blossoms, and tries to pick and pull blooms out of buds. Small children offer us a never ending lesson in patience. The tussles we get into over these basic performances are only the beginning—the forerunner of more serious behavior which *most* children will exhibit at one time or another. The relationship we establish in these first encounters will work for—or against—us when we have to deal with lying, pilfering, squabbling, biting and other acts of aggression. Looking at her innocent beautiful baby, it is hard for a mother to imagine that she will ever have to deal with such transgressions, but to be forewarned is to be forearmed.

Biting

When I speak to parent groups I sometimes say, "At some point before your child reaches the age of six he is likely to bite another human being. When it happens, if you remember what I am telling you, you may be able to take it in your stride. If you express horror, shock or anger; if you shout, shake or punish your child severely, you may create a mountain out of what might have been a molehill. On the other hand, if you can say to yourself, 'Well, she said it would happen and here it is. Now what do I do?' you will be able to devote your energy to corrective

treatment. Certainly I am not suggesting that you should ignore it when your child bites — or treat it lightly. Doctors tell us that a human bite, when it breaks the skin, can be more serious than that of an animal. You must impress on the child that this is something you will not tolerate.

"Of all the behavioral problems the parents or teachers of a preschool child may encounter probably biting invokes the strongest feelings. Everyone's personality, pride and defensive mechanisms are drawn into the maelstrom of emotions.

"This is demonstrated in the following story."

A piercing cry shattered the peace of the infant-toddler nursery. "Carmina!" the teacher shouted, hastening over to the source of the outcry. "You have hurt poor little Jana again! I've told you and told you not to bite!"

Carmina, twenty one months old, quickly bit her own arm, hard enough to draw blood! Jana had teeth marks on her cheek, and even more frightening, on her eyelid.

"Take Jana to the infirmary," Kitty directed an aide, "and Carmina, you come with me." Grasping her hand firmly, she took her to the director's office to report the incident.

"Did you notice what happened just before she bit Jana?" the director asked.

"Yes, I was looking right at her," Kitty replied. "Jana had just climbed up on her feet and was starting to take a step (you know she has just begun to walk) when she fell down and cried. I saw Carmina run toward her but I thought she was going to help her up. Instead, she bit her! I never knew a small child could be so vicious!"

"This is the third time she has bitten another child this week," the director commented, "and each time it was when that child cried. It almost seems as if it is the crying that sets her off. Keep her close to you for the rest of the morning. Her mother will be coming soon, and I will talk to her about this."

"You wanted to see me?" Mrs. Salvucci asked anxiously when she came into the office. "Didn't my husband send the check?"

"Oh, I'm sure he did," the director answered. "I asked you to come in to talk about what is going on with Carmina. Three times this week she has bitten another child!"

The young mother, immediately on the defensive, stated flatly, "Then I'll keep her home!"

"That wasn't what I had in mind when I asked to see you," Marsha replied. "We want to help Carmina learn to play with other children and not hurt them. She is a very bright little girl and with the exception of this one problem she seems to get along well at school. Something is causing her frustration — and she is acting instinctively. I think you would be wise to ask your pediatrician about it. Whatever is troubling her may well be aggravated when your new baby comes. How much longer is it?"

"Three months," was the tight-lipped response. "There is nothing wrong with my Carmina. We never have any trouble with her at home — and that's where I intend to keep her." Terminating the conversation abruptly, she left in a huff.

Recognizing that the problem — and the responsibility — was more than she wanted to cope with alone, Marsha called Ellen, her area director to discuss the problem.

"I have a hunch that she will bring her back tomorrow," said Ellen. "I am planning to come to your school anyway, if she is there I will observe Carmina and then try again to talk with her mother. Perhaps we will need to get her father in, too."

The next day Carmina's father brought her in and left quickly, without mentioning the previous day's episode. When Ellen came she sat where she could watch Carmina who was playing happily in the doll corner. There was a low divider between her and the area where the babies were playing on a carpet. When one of the infants cried, Carmina was over the divider faster than anyone could stop her and a teacher barely caught her as she approached the baby, mouth open ready to bite. Reinforced by this additional observation, the director was able to persuade the parents to seek professional help.

If we can accept the fact that biting is common with young children, what can we do about it?

First, consider the age of the child. The infant bites because his gums hurt—and to bite down hard on something gives relief. Whether the object is inanimate or alive is not part of his concern.

With the toddlers and the two's, it may be just a social advance. At this early age little children express their desire to make contact as quickly with a push, shove, slap, or squeeze as they do with a pat or a kiss. They really are not able to distinguish between what is loving and what hurts.

Carmina's behavior went beyond the usual biting problems of toddlers.

When a four or five-year-old bites it is even more important to look for the cause. This is the manifestation of a deeper problem. Something is going on in this child's life which is disturbing him enough to set his world ajar, and like thumb-sucking and masturbation, his behavior is a means for express-ing his anxiety.

My first recommendation is to talk it over with the chronic biter's parents. Since the problem is usually in the home, be prepared to meet with anger and a defensive attitude. What you are suggesting is really an attack on their qualifications for parenting—and that is hard to accept. If you can be calm and objective, reassuring them that this is not unusual behavior and avoiding any attempt to place blame, you may be able to get at the real source. You may say, "This does not mean that your child is a monster, but at the present time it is enough of a problem so that I need to be concerned with protecting the other children. Perhaps you need to cut back on the time he is spending here." Or, "I think I will have to ask you to keep him home until he gets through this stage." What often happens is that if a working mother can arrange to take a few days off from work and give her child more of her attention, the situation may resolve itself. Or, if the child realizes that he is staying home because of the biting, and he misses his friends at school, he may exert the necessary self control.

The answer to the problem should be worked out through a cooperative, thoughtful effort on both sides. Young children are not able to put themselves in another's place. They have no sense of inflicting hurt. At the time of the incident, the teacher has to deal with her own emotions of anger and concern and with the feelings of both of the children involved.

The child who was bitten should have immediate comfort and care. After thoroughly washing the injury and swabbing it with a disinfectant, the teacher might give him some ice cubes wrapped in a paper towel to hold against it. Then something must be done about the offender.

It is better to get down to his level where you can look right in his eyes, hold him firmly and talk about it. Do not go into a verbal tirade about his being naughty or bad, or that he will not have any friends. You waste your emotional energy and it usually falls on deaf ears. Do say "It hurt Johnny when you bit him. See, your teeth made a mark on his arm. Teeth are for eating food, but you MAY NOT BITE PEOPLE!"

You may remove him from the group temporarily, but not in a way which humiliates him or embarrasses him. It is important that the biter doesn't win. Don't let him have the toy they were fighting over.

Sometimes it works to place a toddler in a play pen, explaining that "you will have to play by yourself for a while because you hurt Johnny."

When all else fails, and if you absolutely must keep the child in the center, the only safe, effective method is to have one adult within arm's reach every minute of the day, ready to anticipate the act and move fast. It need not be the same person — different staff members can be assigned fifteen minute periods of guard duty, but you do have an obligation to protect the other children.

This is probably one of the most difficult problems to resolve in the entire scope of child care. Very little has been written about it because the "experts" are reluctant to offer pat answers — and indeed there are none, since everything depends on the circumstances. However, there is one point on which I

believe there would be general agreement. You never, never try
to "teach" the child not to bite by showing him that it hurts.
Children look up to grown ups who are caring for them. If an
adult bites, the message conveyed is that this is acceptable
behavior. Such a simplified attack on the problem is really a cop-
out, a sign that the parent or teacher is not willing to expend the
time or energy to *help children see the sense in acting in a certain
way*.

Lying

Let me state unequivocally, at the outset, that I do not
believe that children under the age of four lie and/or steal. They
may make statements which, by adult standards, are untrue,
and they pick up whatever attracts them because they have not
reached the age when there is a sharp distinction between
"yours" and "mine". They cannot deal with this as "right" or
"wrong". It would be hard to say when this awareness is born —
maturity cannot be measured in exact time spans — but it is
better to give children the benefit of the doubt than to accuse
them unjustly. This was demonstrated in the following
incidents.

"Oh, Miss Jackson!" Mrs. Foster wailed over the phone.
"What am I going to do with Leslie? She tells such awful lies. I
have tried to tell her it is wicked but she doesn't listen to me!"

Leslie was Mrs. Foster's only child, born when her parents
were past the usual child bearing age, and these calls were an
almost daily occurrence, so with a resigned shrug of her
shoulders Miss Jackson asked, "What kind of stories does she
tell?"

"Well," Leslie's mother responded indignantly, "Yesterday
when we were having lunch she told me this crazy story about
the pony eating his cart. When I tried to tell her I knew it was a
make-believe story she insisted that it was true! I'm sure I ought
to curb this right now, but I don't know what to do. I hate to
punish her!"

"Would it surprise you to know?" Miss Jackson responded
with a laugh, "that she was telling the truth? You may not have
noticed it but Queenie's stable is divided. She stands on one side

and the basket cart is on the other. Yesterday she did reach over and take a bit out of the rim. It was the main topic of conversation for the whole day! Of course she wanted to tell you about it!"

"Well, I never!" Mrs. Foster breathed, totally at a loss for words.

Young children, especially before they have developed a conscience, which occurs somewhere around the age of five, are also in the process of developing an imagination. Language is a newly discovered tool with which they enjoy experimenting. Some of their stories are pure fantasy, and should be treated as such, but parents must be careful not to jump to that conclusion, as is plain in the next incident.

Truth is Stranger Than Fiction

Virginia's mother was trying very hard to be a good parent. She read all of the books and magazine articles, and called upon Marlene, the nursery school director, frequently, for advice. One day after dropping off her child, she stopped in with a complaint.

"I'm really worried about Virginia," she began. "Lately she has been telling me the wildest stories. I know what you have said about children's imaginations, but what should I do when I know it must be a lie? If I pretend to believe it, won't I be teaching her that lying is acceptable?"

"What is her latest story?" Marlene asked. "Perhaps we can figure out what you should have said."

"It was really kind of gruesome," Virginia's mother said, with a shudder. "All about making snakes, and putting them on a stick, and cooking them over a fire, and eating them! How can she dream up such ridiculous tales?"

"Did you ever go to camp when you were a child?" Marlene asked.

"No, but what has that to do with Virginia's lying?" her mother replied with an annoyed expression.

"Well, it happens that Jill, Virginia's teacher, worked in a day camp last summer and learned how to make bread twists. She asked me if she could try it with her children, and apparently it was successful!"

"What is a bread twist?" Mrs. Taylor queried, still suspicious of being put off.

"Well, first they mixed up a batch of good stiff biscuit dough. The children were able to help with that. Then Jill gave each of the children a piece of dough and showed them how to roll it between their hands to make a snake, just as they do when they play with clay. Then they wrapped the snake round and round the end of a stick and held it over a charcoal fire, turning it slowly. When it was puffed up and golden brown, she helped them slip it off carefully. Next they dropped a piece of butter and some jelly down the coiled bread and they ate them. They were delicious! Why don't you come over some day and they can do it again. It does take two or three adults to help with children that young!"

These two amusing anecdotes stress the fact that the truth *is* sometimes stranger than fiction, and adults should be cautious about making accusations or punishing a child without further inquiry.

It does no great harm to play along for a bit with comments such as, "Oh, that is very interesting. Tell me more about it." But when it is obvious that the story is a fantasy, it is also important to make that distinction with the child. You certainly do not punish him for it; fantasy is *not* lying. It is creative story telling. What, then, is lying?

Why Do They Tell Lies?

When a person, child or adult, consciously and deliberately changes the truth in order to avoid punishment, to win unearned praise, to get someone else into trouble or to gain attention—that is lying. When this behavior becomes a habit, serious trouble is looming ahead.

You teach by example. Parents are the child's first and most consistent teachers. Teachers and preachers come and go, and have varying influences on their subjects, but parents are there year after year. As they struggle through each of the developmental stages, hoping that the next one will be easier, they can never lose sight of the inescapable fact that they provide the role models after which a child will pattern his personality and character. If he hears and sees his parents twisting the truth to serve their own ends, what will he learn?

Joan hears her mother call her father's office to say he is sick, when Joan knows he is going to the ball game.

"That dented fender happened in another accident, but put it down," Hans hears his father tell the insurance adjuster as he slips him a bill. "I might as well collect on it while I have the chance. I pay big enough premiums!"

"I'm so sorry, I won't be able to take my turn helping at the church thrift shop tomorrow," Mrs. Hinds says on the phone. "I have just heard that I have company coming."

"Who's coming, Mother?" Alice cries with excited anticipation.

"No one," her mother replies, exasperated at being overheard. "I want to go in town tomorrow to have lunch with my friends. I might even get that new doll you have been wanting—so you didn't hear me make that phone call," she finishes with a conspiratorial smile.

What does twelve-year-old Kenneth learn when he hears his mother tell the ticket seller at the movie, "He's only eleven. He's tall for his age."

Sometimes we make it almost impossible for a child to tell the truth.

Maureen gasped in dismay when she entered the living room and saw her favorite vase in pieces on the floor in a puddle of water and scattered flowers. In one corner of the room was Georgie's large red ball. "George!" yelled Maureen.

The kitchen door opened, and slowly the five-year-old entered, his eyes avoiding the broken vase.

With her eyes snapping with anger, and in a voice shaking with fury, Maureen shouted, "That is the vase Aunt Joanna gave me. It is a very valuable vase. Did you or didn't you break it?"

What is Georgie going to do? He doesn't have to be told that if he admits to breaking the vase, punishment is going to be swift and painful. If he thinks there is any chance of blaming the catastrophe on the cat, his baby sister, or a rush of wind, he is going to do it.

What then, could Maureen do instead? She doesn't have to disguise the fact that she is upset, and she does have to find out if Georgie really was responsible, but hopefully with some self-control, in a voice more troubled than enraged. This greatly increases the chances of Georgie's telling the truth. Then comes the tricky part. It is important to acknowledge that telling the truth is hard. Suppose Maureen were to say, "Thank you. I know it wasn't easy to tell me that. I'm proud of you for telling the truth. Nevertheless, you did break the rule about playing ball in the living room, and the vase got broken. I have to punish you for that, so you will remember and not do it again." The punishment would then be something directed to the actual offense, and tempered by Georgie's telling the truth.

If you can accept the notion that discipline is trying to teach the child *"the sense of acting in a certain way"*, you must carefully build an understanding of how important it is that people must be able to trust you. You explain — not once, but again and again, in varying words — "If you don't tell the truth, someday when it is really important for people to believe you, they won't."

You read stories that point up this lesson — "The Boy Who Cried Wolf," for example. You discuss together TV shows in which this point is made. Only when he really understands the value of one's "good name" will your child *"see the sense"* of telling the truth, even when it hurts.

If, in spite of your best efforts, your child repeatedly lies, look for the underlying cause. Often lying is a signal for attention. Melinda lies about her father's job, or the exotic presents she received for her birthday, in a pathetic attempt to win friends. Tommy tells a whopper about where he was when he came home two hours late, which may be saying, "I have to remind you that I am here. You have been too busy lately to notice me."

Stealing

Stealing is a very close relative of lying. When the first attempts to extend the limits of truth are ignored, or accepted with inappropriate punishment, it is an easy next step to stealing. As with all misdemeanors the age of the culprit is the first consideration. Every nursery school teacher soon learns that there are some children who need to turn out their pockets daily before going home. They will have a collection of small pieces of games and puzzles, little cars and other memorabilia. If it belongs to the school it is a matter of drawing a line between "what is mine to play with here—and what I brought from home." If it has been taken from another child it calls for a different conversation, but it would be a mistake to make a big deal of it in the beginning. Repeated offenses would suggest that there might be a cause which should be explored.

The older child who is fully aware of what he is doing when he slips a few candy bars, or a small toy into his pocket in the store and walks out without paying is again testing, not his parents but the rules of society. When it is discovered, it is wise to take immediate action. The parent need not yell, scream, or threaten with the cops. A calm, matter of fact, but very positive approach will be more effective. First, he must go back to the store, admit his misdemeanor and make restitution. Punishment should follow but the real challenge to the parent is to try to discover the reason behind the act.

Just as your children learn from your bad examples, you can also teach what is right. Most parents have innumerable chances to show their children that you just do not take or keep what is not yours.

Sally and her friend took their children to a movie and to the ice cream parlor afterwards. Sally paid the check as they left, at the same time continuing her conversation with her friend. Before they reached the car she stopped short and said, "Wait a minute. I just realized I only paid two dollars and twenty-five cents. That can't have been right, for four of us. Why, Jimmy's banana split alone was one-fifty."

The harried clerk watched as the entire procession of moms and kids came back into the store. Patiently, Sally explained the mistake. The clerk, busy with other customers, thought that she was returning to complain about an overcharge. When he realized that Sally was trying to rectify an undercharged bill, he grinned in relief and gratitude. The children listened wide-eyed throughout the entire exchange. A much more positive lesson was achieved than had Sally simply told everyone to wait by the car.

Unacceptable Language

"How would you like to go with me to feed the ducks?" the young teacher asked Terri, a pixie-like three-year-old.

Trustingly, Terri took the teacher's hand and they walked to the edge of the pond, carrying a bag of stale bread.

As they approached, the ducks came swimming rapidly to the shore and waddled out of the pond, quacking loudly. Terrified, Terri literally climbed up the teacher's legs screaming, "Jesus Christ, the fuckin' ducks will get me!"

Does it shock you to think of a three-year-old child using these words? Of course it does, because at your age, and with your life experience, you have acquired knowledge of their meaning and an attitude toward their use. To Terri, who had been placed in the day care center by a social worker, such words were as commonplace as bread and butter, chair or window. They were the common vernacular of her home and the neighborhood. They were the words people use to express fear, anger or distress.

Although the teacher was young and inexperienced, she

reacted wisely. Ignoring the explosive language she directed her attention to comforting and soothing Terri — assuring the frightened little girl that the ducks would not harm her. When Terri finally was coaxed to hold out a piece of bread, her terror turned to glee as she watched the ducks gobble down their food and waddle back into the pond.

Later in the day, this young teacher described the incident to her director and asked whether she had handled it properly. "Yes," the director said, "especially since this was Terri's first day. Her language does pose a problem. If she uses words like that very often the other children are likely to copy her, and if they repeat them at home I will probably have complaints from the parents."

"What on earth will you tell them?" she was asked.

"Well, I will probably say, 'We are aware of the situation and are working on it. We believe that in time we can teach Terri that such words are unacceptable, but we think it is important to do this without making her feel guilty because she doesn't know that they are wrong.'

"Now," she went on, addressing her teachers, "let's think about how we *can* deal with it here in school. I suggest that we should move cautiously. This is a case where we remind ourselves of one of the basic rules of learning: start where the learner is. Our children, when they come to this center, bring with them more than a blanket and an extra set of clothing...they also bring values and customs which they have learned from their environment. We certainly cannot tell Terri that she is naughty or that those words are bad, because she probably hears her parents say them frequently. Instead we will have to be creative in thinking of ways to change her language patterns. I don't really see this as a discipline problem, because there was no deliberate intent. If Terri were older and was doing this as a means of getting attention it would be a different matter. Helping this child will be a *'slow, bit-by-bit, time-consuming process'*.

"As teachers we will have to work on our own feelings and attitudes. We, too, bring more than our education and book learning to this situation; each of us has an ingrained set of values which we have been acquiring over the years.

"Now, back to Terri. The day will come when we can tell her

that some words are not acceptable here. Give her some language that will serve her need such as: 'You are angry!' 'Tell Johnny you are mad!' 'You are frightened!'—say 'I'm scared!'

"You can tell Craig that you wanted that toy—ask him to give it to you after he has a turn."

Bathroom Talk

There is a stage—usually at about four—when children are addicted to bathroom talk.

"My kids are in that stage," the teacher of the four's piped up. "They get so silly! Last week Henry was giving them rides in the pony cart and when he was finished he said to me, 'All these kids want to talk about is what comes after Howdy!'"

"There is an explanation," the director replied. "These children are just discovering the power of language. They have a great need to play with words, roll them off their tongues, and when they discover a few that will incite a response, either from their peers or a listening adult, they use them to the hilt! That is why we sing songs, and recite poems that have a lot of syllables without any particular meaning. It always amazes me that they learn them so quickly. When Mary Poppins was popular even the very young children could rattle off 'Supercalafragilistic-expialadocious' and I still can't remember it!"

I knew one teacher who kept a copy of Edward Lear's Nonsense Alphabet close by and when language began to get raunchy she would gather the children around her and read the verses slowly, taking time for a good laugh over each one.

Nonsense Alphabet

a

A was once an apple pie,
Pidy,
Widy,
Tidy,
Pidy,
Nice insidy,
Apple-pie!

b

B was once a little bear,
Beary
Wary,
Hairy,
Beary,
Taky cary,
Little bear!

c

C was once a little cake,
Caky,
Baky,
Maky,
Caky,
Taky caky,
Little cake!

We can excuse vile language from children who are too young to have learned the meaning of the words they use so gliby. What about the elementary school child who does know the difference? We are seeing this comprehension at earlier stages than ever before.

A fourth grade teacher took a bold approach. We might say she met fire with fire.

"Teacher, Vena called me an asshole," Mary Alice complained.

"That wasn't very nice of her. I can see it made you feel bad. Why don't you sit down and work on this puzzle with Shelley?" Miss Jones answered, in a matter of fact tone.

Quietly, Miss Jones took Vena aside.

"You called Mary Alice an asshole," she stated.

Vena's eyes opened wide with horror! She couldn't believe that her teacher had actually said that word.

"Would you call me an asshole?" Miss Jones asked.

"No!" Vena shook her head violently.

"Would you call your mother an asshole?"

"No way! She'd kill me!" was the quick response.

"Would you call Mr. Vanni, the principal, an asshole?" was the next question.

The mere thought brought such a shocked expression to Vena's face that Miss Jones had difficulty maintaining her serious expression.

"Well, if you wouldn't say it to any of these people, it must not be a very good word and I don't think you want to say it to your friends."

Miss Jones dropped the matter there. She did not berate Vena, or require her to apologize to Mary Alice. This child was in the fourth grade. She knew that her language was "off limits" but she enjoyed the reaction she knew would be forthcoming when she teased Mary Alice.

Tom, a sixth grader, had sprinkled the four letter words of the street liberally through his daily conversation. He knew what he was doing. In a sense he was establishing his identity as a tough kid. In his case, there was only one way to respond. A flat statement.... "Your language is offensive. There are plenty of good words in the English language to express your feelings and if you don't know any, I will help you find some, but I cannot let you talk that way in school. What you are doing is just as bad as punching and hitting. You are attacking the ears and the senses of the people around you and so you are interfering with their rights. If you continue to talk this way deliberately we will have to find some way of punishing you."

Although the incidents described happened in schools, the problem is just as prevalent in the home. Some parents take a "Do as I say, not as I do" attitude, punishing their children for using the words they utter frequently themselves. Others overreact when their children repeat offensive words that they have heard on the outside. A calm, matter of fact statement, "Daddy and I don't like those words. We don't use them and we don't want you to" will be more effective than an angry scene. Children are quick to recognize and capitalize on behavior that will stir up excitement.

Throwing

The nursery school teacher was interrupted in her conversation with another teacher by a piercing scream. A three-year-old came running toward her, blood streaming from a gash over her eye.

Alarmed, and feeling somewhat guilty because she had not seen the incident, Sandy picked Sara Jane up, crying "What happened?"

"Dana hit her with a rock!" the other children volunteered.

"Dana, I'll see you later," Sandy said in an angry voice as she hurried into the building for first aid for Sara Jane.

When she returned with Sara Jane, who was proudly displaying a bandaged head, she took Dana by the hand and sat down beside him. "That was a naughty thing you did, Dana," she began. "You hurt Sara Jane! That stone almost hit her in the eye. It could have made her blind! You know what I have said about throwing stones! Why did you do it?"

Dana, whose anxiety had been growing while Sara Jane was gone, burst into tears. "I didn't throw the stone at Sara Jane!" he sobbed. "She is my friend. I wouldn't hurt her! I just picked up the stone and throwed it. When I grow big I want to be a baseball pitcher, and Daddy said to practice throwing!"

"Oh, I see," Sandy smiled. "Well, throwing is fun—and it is good exercise, but I'm sure you can see that we have to be careful what we throw and where we throw it."

Using her imagination, and with the approval of the director, Sandy set up several games which gave the children legitimate reasons for throwing.

She brought an old bedspread from home and suspended it on a rope between two posts and painted a target on it. The little ones were satisfied with just throwing a ball against it, but the older children practiced for accuracy and kept score.

She created an area where the children could throw wet sand against the side of the building—a very different throwing experience.

She made a game of tossing a ball into a wastebasket, emphasizing the difference between tossing and throwing.

In an open area beyond the fence in the playground, she set up a tin can as a target and the children tried to knock it off with stones. In all of her games, the rules were explicit. All participants were lined up well behind the person who was throwing. Talking about and making the rules governing safety was an important part of each game.

Frequently, when we are disturbed by an act which would be legitimate under different circumstances, we can substitute another activity which will satisfy the child's need. In that case, we can say, "I cannot let you throw stones — or play with big sticks — but I know it is something you like to do. Let's see if we can think of ways to do it without hurting anyone!" Given the challenge, children can often exceed adults in the imaginative games they will contrive!

Sandy was dealing with a child who had been hit by accident. Explaining the need to be careful and then offering acceptable ways to throw things, without risk, was an excellent way to handle that particular situation.

However, some children do throw things with the intention of hitting someone and a desire to hurt. In many cases the act is instinctive — not premeditated — but that doesn't make it less dangerous. It is important to deal with this firmly and consistently while the child is young. When he gets older and stronger, if he is permitted to resolve his conflicts with violence, he may well continue that pattern through adolescence and into adulthood.

The young child who has not learned how to deal with his strong feelings needs to be able to lean on the security of knowing that someone will stop him before he hurts anyone. When an adult says, "I will not let you hurt Susy," it is comforting — not threatening.

Then he is ready to recognize that feelings are not bad in themselves — it is what we do with them — and that there are ways to let them out which will not get him into trouble.

Temper Tantrums

Probably one of the most frightening behavior problems a parent or teacher encounters is the uncontrolled display of temper. Even a tiny baby can frighten the wits out of his parents by holding his breath until he turns purple, and that is the forerunner of increasing displays of temper. The toddler usually uses his vocal chords to make known his demands.

What can you do with a child who is screaming? Clearly this is one time when the firm, calm, direct approach is ineffective.

To say "your screaming is annoying me and disturbing others" will not make much of an impression if the child who is bellowing cannot hear you. Diversionary tactics are required — but what?

You can offer a toy — which may be snatched and thrown across the room.

You can try to hug and soothe — and may be bruised in the process. Rosalie, a teacher who contributed several stories to this book, told of a technique which she jokingly called the "water treatment."

"José was a volatile four-year-old," she recounted, "who could scream longer and louder than any other child I have ever known. One day I put on my most concerned, solicitous expression and offered him a glass of water. I expected that he might dash it out of my hand but instead, with a surprised look he accepted it and gulped it down. Since he couldn't swallow and scream at the same time, I had a chance to talk. 'Your throat must really hurt,' I said, soothingly. 'Now you just have a nice drink and it will feel better. As soon as you have finished we will go find a carrot for Peter Rabbit.' It worked! That time and the next, and the next! My moment of joy came when I saw José open his mouth and start to scream. Suddenly he stopped — went over to the sink and got his own drink of water!"

Recently, when I was sitting on a plane waiting for take-off, a little fellow, rebelling against the restriction of a seat belt, tuned up. As the crescendo of his screams increased, the other passengers were shooting looks of sympathy and annoyance at his embarrassed mother. The flight attendant must have learned Rosalie's secret. He approached with a glass of water — and it achieved the desired results!

When parents are faced with this problem they should first be aware that there are different kinds of temper tantrums. There are the deliberately contrived scenes where a child throws himself on the floor and kicks and screams in order to have his own way. Whether he wants a candy bar, a new toy, or the desired seat by the window in the family car, it becomes a power struggle, a battle of wills, and if he is allowed to win this game, it takes on new dimensions each time it is played. These tantrums usually end abruptly once the desired goal is achieved. If the parent gives in the demonstration stops. It is hard to turn your back on him if he puts on his act in public and his actions are drawing an audience, but whenever it is possible this is the best method.

Much more serious are the temper tantrums which take over a child when he is seized by uncontrollable anger. In such a state he is not responsible for his own actions, and may cause serious injury to himself or others or mindless destruction of property. If such tantrums are not curbed in the early years of his life the child becomes more and more of a menace — and less receptive to help.

In this case the attitude of the adult he sees as a role model may play an important part. We have all known men who seem to be proud of their tempers. "Better keep out of my way when you see fire in my eye!" they will say without realizing that the message they are conveying is "Look how big and important I am! See what power I have! Everyone is afraid of me!" Some wives view this as "Macho" and can be heard saying, "My husband has a terrible temper! When he is mad we all clear out of his way!" It is not surprising that children who witness this behavior never learn to make an effort to control their own displays of temper.

Dealing with a violent temper is never easy. In the two parent family, a consistent approach, discussed and agreed upon by both parents will be most effective. In today's world where the single parent is often trying to maintain a dual role the problem is even more heartbreaking. We hear a lot about parents who abuse their children physically or emotionally, but very little from the parents who are ashamed to admit that they are actually afraid of their children. A husky well-developed five-year-old who discovers that he can intimidate his mother is in a very scary position. He finds himself behind the controls before he has learned to fly. If someone doesn't stop him he is heading for serious trouble!

It takes enormous effort and self control for the parent or teacher to provide the troubled child with the reassurance of calm, steady, consistent support. Saying "I will not let you do that" is like offering a rope to a drowning victim. Offering positive reinforcement, in the form of justifiable praise when he does succeed in avoiding a scene or exerting self control will enable him to pull himself up that rope, whereas yelling back at

him, responding with an anger as great as his own, or physically punishing him will be like pushing him down deeper into the depths of his own uncontrolled feelings.

Adults must be objective, not emotional. They need to start when the child is young enough so they can control him physically, not by spanking but holding him firmly, while speaking in a calm soothing voice. With children old enough to comprehend, a discussion of the problem can be held later, when the child is calm.

For example: "We had a bad time because you lost your temper when Gary wouldn't let you be first. He made you mad and you tried to hurt him. No one has the right to hurt another person. Such behavior is not acceptable in this house (school)."

"Well, I've tried all this," weary parents will say. "For a whole month I have been a model of restraint, but nothing seems to have done any good. My child still flies off the handle at the drop of a hat."

The circumstances leading to the behavior probably had been building up for much longer than a month — and the glue which will mend the cracks — calm, quiet, firm, consistent support — will have to be applied, as the old song says, "not for just a day, not for just a year — but always!"

CHAPTER 9

Move Over for the New Baby

The nursery room was quiet and peaceful. The children were all asleep on their cots and Louise, their teacher, was just settling down for a moment's rest when suddenly Sheila, a precocious young lady of three, sat straight up on her cot.

"When that baby comes out of my mother's stomach I am going to shake her — and shake her — and shake her!" she announced in a determined voice, demonstrating her thoughts with violent movements of her arms.

Louise moved quietly over to sit on the floor beside Sheila's cot. "Tell me about it," she whispered, "but we will have to talk softly so we won't wake the other children."

"Well, if SHE thinks she's going to give that baby MY crib, and all those dresses that were mine when I was a baby — well, SHE'S NOT!"

Louise knew about the pending blessed event. Everyone knew about it. Sheila had been walking around for weeks with her stomach thrust out, telling the children she was going to have a baby. Her mother had taken her into her confidence almost as soon as she had received the initial news from the doctor, and that had been a mistake. A small child's sense of time is narrow — everything is in the NOW — and the anticipation was too much to bear. It was plain that her mother had painted what she thought was a rosy picture, but Sheila had different ideas.

Dr. Volta Hall, the psychiatrist mentioned earlier, once explained a child's feeling of displacement with the following story.

How Would You Feel?

"Imagine," he said to a group of teachers and parents, "that you are a bride of one year. Your husband has adored you, doted on you, admired your every act. You have been Queen, the first Lady, the apple of his eye. Now picture him sitting down with his arms around you saying 'Darling, I have wonderful news for you. Some day soon I am going away for a few days. My mother will stay with you while I am gone, and when I come back I will have a surprise— a NEW BRIDE! Won't that be wonderful? She can sleep in your bed in my room—and you can have a nice big bed and room all of your own. She can wear all of those pretty dresses you had when you were a bride. You can help me take care of her, and when she has been here a while and gets used to us, you can play with her! Isn't that going to be fun!'"

This is the approach so often taken when parents tell their offspring of the advent of a new member in the family. On the surface it may seem sensible, but if we stop to think about the bride's feelings we can begin to empathize with the child who has been receiving all of his parents' attention and is told to "move over". It is ridiculous to imagine that the news will be accepted with delight. It is naive for parents to rule out the possibility of jealousy, lest they fail to notice when gentle patting turns to surreptitious pinching.

Having been forewarned by this story, Matty and Christa found a better way to help their four-year-old son adjust to the arrival of his baby sister. She was still sleeping in a bassinette when they discussed the need for a new crib in Matthew's presence.

"I guess we'll just have to buy a new crib," Christa said.

"Yes, I suppose we will," Matty replied. "Well, there goes the money we had been saving for a vacation."

Matthew who had been listening attentively burst forth with, "Dad, I have a great idea! We can give Ashley my crib and I can sleep on a big bed!"

"That is very generous of you," Matty replied, "But are you sure you are ready to sleep in another room — all by yourself?"

"Sure," was the confident reply, "and you know that bathtub Mum used to wash me in when I was a baby is still down in the cellar. Ashley could have that too!" Instead of feeling disgruntled and displaced Matthew became a solicitous protective big brother.

Sometimes a child who appears to have weathered the arrival of a new baby without any serious reactions will suffer pangs of sibling rivalry when that baby suddenly becomes "cute"; when she takes that first step, says that first word, and is suddenly the center of attention. Billy was a prime example of this delayed reaction.

Delayed Feelings of Jealousy

"We are having some problems with Billy," Miss Simmons reported to Mrs. Ash. "He has been doing a lot of biting lately — and he seems to be focusing on one particular child. Could you come a little early today when you pick him up so we can talk it over?"

When Mrs. Ash came, her husband was with her. "We have been having a terrible time with Billy at home," she reported. "He has always been such a good kid, and lately he has been obnoxious. He is sneaky, lies, cries, and whines a lot. We didn't realize you were having trouble too, but we are really concerned. Do you suppose there is something physically wrong with him? Why would a child's personality change so drastically? Should we take him to a psychiatrist?"

"How old is your little one?" Miss Simmons asked.

"Oh, she's fifteen months, and such a doll!" her mother replied, glowing. "She has just started walking, and she is so cute, toddling along and falling down every third step."

"Do you think that could be Billy's problem?" was the next question.

"Why would that happen now?" asked Mr. Ash. "We thought we might have problems when she first came home from the hospital, but Billy seemed to accept her very well."

"It is not uncommon for this delayed reaction to occur when the new baby begins to be really cute, and everyone is admiring each new advance in her growth," Miss Simmons said. "I have never seen her. What does she look like?"

Melissa has adorable dimples," her mother responded enthusiastically, "and blonde curls, and the brightest blue eyes! She does attract a lot of attention, even from strangers when we go out. She is a real ham — plays up to everyone. She bats her eyes at the men like a little flirt!"

"It may be just a coincidence," Miss Simmons went on. "We should be careful not to jump to conclusions, but the child Billy has bitten several times has blonde, curly hair and blue eyes. It has reached the point where she starts screaming when she sees him coming."

"Oh, that's awful!" Mrs. Ash exclaimed in shocked tones. "The poor thing! It's a wonder her mother hasn't complained!"

"She has," Miss Simmons said ruefully. "She is a very sensible, understanding person, but I would hate to have to explain one more bite. For the past two days I have had someone staying within arm's reach of Billy, until I could talk to you and see if we could find out what was going on."

Mr. Ash had been quietly listening to most of this, but now he spoke up. "It seems to me we have been pretty blind. I don't know why we didn't see for ourselves what was happening. Anyway, I can see what we have to do. First of all, we stop making so much of the baby in Billy's presence — and we will warn the relatives to tone down their admiration! Then we'll spend some extra time with Billy, let him know he's still very special to us. Maybe we could leave the baby with a sitter and take Billy off with us for the day. He loves to go into the city — ride the elevators, eat in a restaurant. We haven't done that since Melissa was born. What I want to know now is whether we should speak to Billy about biting?"

"Not yet," Miss Simmons replied. "He is a very bright boy. He knows what he is doing is wrong — and I think if he learns that I have told you his guilt will only make matters worse. Let's see what happens when you can put some of your ideas into effect. I will keep on top of the situation here."

Jealousy of a new baby will crop up in different ways — and at different times, but it always stems from the same source — the feeling that the child has been pushed aside and is no longer of first importance to his parents. Danny had succeeded in concealing his anxiety from his parents but it did show up in his behavior at school.

Covering Up Jealousy

"Is anything unusual going on in your home?" Miss Lawson asked in a phone call to Danny's mother. "Danny has been acting in a very disruptive way for a week now — not at all like his usual self."

"Why no, we haven't seen anything different at home," Mrs. Jacobs replied. "I'm sorry if he is giving you so much trouble. I will talk about it when he comes home."

"Please don't. Let's give it a little time and see if we can find out what's going on. Do you think it might have anything to do with the new baby?"

"I'm sure it isn't that," Mrs. Jacobs replied emphatically. "He adores her. He runs straight to her when he comes in the house and is so gentle and loving with her."

That very afternoon Mrs. Jacobs called Miss Lawson. Her voice was trembling. "I'm literally shaking," she reported. "I can't believe what just happened. I remember what you had said at our last parents meeting about ways of helping children air their true feelings, so I asked Danny if he would like to write a letter to his grandmother. Of course, I was doing the writing, but let me read to you what he said.

"'Dear Nanny,

There is a greenhouse at my school. Behind the greenhouse is a bush with poison berries. I am going to pick some of the poison berries and give them to Suzanne.'"

It may seem presumptuous for a teacher who does not have any children of her own to be offering advice to a mother, but teachers deal with many children and a wide range of problems. They can be more objective about looking at causes and seeking solutions. They can apply their learning and note the results. If one thing doesn't work, they can try another approach.

Parents are more emotionally involved when a problem of behavior crops up. Their experience is limited to their own children, and very often they have never read or studied child development, so they do not have the comfort that comes from knowing that certain behavior is to be expected at a certain age. This is one area in which they can benefit from the advice of teachers who have studied normal growth and development. Parents and teachers can learn from each other; they can look at behavior from a different perspective.

Miss Lawson suggested a simple technique to Danny's mother—a tool to help him express the thoughts that were troubling him. She stressed that it was important for her to maintain her position as a "non-person"—to convey the impression that she was just a machine recording his thoughts. If Mrs. Jacobs had stopped in shocked disbelief and berated Danny for having such wicked ideas, she would have slammed the lid on his emotions, pushing them down inside where they could fester and erupt in another way.

The question arises as to how the mother could be so deceived about Danny. What about the "gentle, loving" child who "adored" his baby sister?

Parents often delude themselves into seeing what they want to see. Children know what their parents want and expect and what pleases them. How often had this mother said to visiting relatives and friends, "It's just wonderful the way Danny loves Suzanne. He can't wait to see her when he comes in."

If Danny really adored the baby, he wouldn't want to hurt her. Isn't it more likely that he runs straight to the baby when he comes in because that's where mother is, so it's the only place where Danny can be noticed by her? It could even be that he is checking to see if the baby is still there. Who knows, she might have vanished as mysteriously as she appeared, leaving Danny supreme again.

What else might have helped ease the pain of this displace-

ment for Danny? Let's go back to one of those key words—
ANTICIPATE.

Make the Child a Part of the Planning

Long before the baby comes, there are some steps you can
take.

First let us consider how you can help a small child
understand that when you take care of something it becomes
more interesting and more important to you as time goes on?

One way is by planting a seed in a cup and watching it grow.
"Those tiny brown seeds aren't very exciting or beautiful," you
can point out, "but we will take care of them, give them water
and sunshine and they will become beautiful flowers or delicious
green peas. Our baby won't look like much at first, but we will
take care of her and she will grow into a big, strong, handsome
child—just like you!"

Books can help. Read stories aloud about sisters and
brothers who have good times together, with comments like,

"Before you can have a brother big enough to do these things with you, we have to have a baby. The baby has eyes and ears and little tiny fingers, but he needs us to take care of him until he can walk and talk and play games with you."

Establish the practice of including the child in some of the things you have to do around the house. Pushing a vacuum cleaner, dusting, sorting laundry and washing dishes are all within the capabilities of a three- or four-year-old. Sure, it takes patience. It is much easier and faster to do it yourself, but it gives him a sense of importance, and when the new baby comes this will be time you spend together — times when that intruder is excluded.

It is a very good idea before the baby comes to develop on a regular basis routine that is special to the child. A "read aloud" time is one suggestion, or regular outings with Daddy. Whatever it is, make time for it, even if the dishes wait! It is important to continue this relationship AFTER the baby arrives. This is a way of saying "Yes, there have been some changes in our family, but YOU are still important to me!"

After the big event, try to be matter of fact about the new baby when the child is present. Without being phony or syrupy sweet, give the older brother or sister your attention and your love. Let him share in the responsibility for the care of the baby as he shows an interest and desire, but do not make it a burden.

Praise the child honestly when he is really helpful — like bringing you a clean diaper, rocking a cradle, holding a bottle, talking or singing to the baby. (In a day care center, the caregivers were amazed to see an infant stop crying when a four-year-old stood by the crib and sang to him. It was a toss-up as to who gained the most — the baby, the child who was being helpful, or the teacher!)

Share with him your memories of his infancy. "When you first came home from the hospital, you were just about this size. You were such a beautiful baby. Daddy and I were so proud of you. I used to sit in that chair right over there and rock you, and sing to you, and look at your perfect little fingernails, and your nice flat little ears." As you say these things, you are letting him feel special while at the same time you draw his attention to the things that make the new baby special.

When you have to make an older child wait because you are changing or feeding the baby, explain, and as soon as possible get back to him.

What has all this to do with discipline? We have already stressed that feelings are at the root of all situations calling for disciplinary action, and jealousy of the new baby is probably the most common cause for unacceptable or unexplainable behavior in very young children. I believe it is a mistake to think that a child will not feel some emotion when he is pushed upstairs by this intruder.

Many children deal with it by reverting to baby ways. They may suck their thumbs, talk baby talk, have toilet accidents or ask for a bottle. This is confusing and sometimes embarrassing for the adults, who react with, "How could you wet your pants! You haven't done that for a long time. You are too big to do such a baby thing!"

"Take your finger out of your mouth. Don't be a baby!"

"No, you can't sit on my lap. You are too big!"

"Of course you can't have your milk in a bottle. What if someone should see you! They would laugh at you — a big girl like you!"

It is irritating, but the parent who gives in and goes along with it — constantly seeking ways to make the displaced child feel important and needed, will find that the problem does not last long.

As parents engage in the arduous but rewarding sojourn of child rearing, there will be many times when they will need to cling to the reassuring phrase from the Good Book "This, too, shall pass!"

CHAPTER 10

Grownups Goof Too!

Can you keep cool, calm and collected when your children cross your grain? Do you stop to weigh your words carefully before admonishing them? Do you maintain a consistently warm, understanding relationship even when they disobey you, talk back, or ignore your directives?

If you can answer "Yes" then fold up your wings and skip on to the next chapter. To the other 99% of my readers, I hope to offer comfort and reassurance. You are not failures as teachers or parents. You are average, normal human beings—with all the usual combinations of strengths and weaknesses. My aim is to help you recognize and acknowledge the problems you may be *creating yourself*—and to plant a few ideas which will help you avoid them.

Working with children is like walking through an open field. On the good days you tread buoyantly over even ground and the grass is soft beneath your feet. And then there comes a day when you stumble into the pitfalls of your own bloopers; when you get caught in a maze of rhetoric and can't find your way out, or when you come smack up against a hard rock of confrontation.

What are some of these common mistakes?

Making Threats You Can't Carry Out

One is making threats you can't carry out.

"Harry Smith, if you don't stop fooling around and get your

81

things on, the school bus will go without you!" the exasperated
teacher hears herself saying when she knows full well Harry
will *have* to be on that bus, even if she has to dress him and carry
him on!

"Now you kids better get this mess cleaned up in five
minutes or we won't go to the show!" mother states in une-
quivocal tones. But she has already paid for the tickets — and
besides she wants to see the show herself. What will she do?

"How many times do I have to tell you to get in here and get
washed?" mother screams at the twins. "Now hurry up — or we
won't go to Grandma's.

If she had been thinking straight she would have known
that her lively four-year-olds would far rather stay home and
play in their own backyard. Her threat would not get them
ready — nor would it put them in a mood to be agreeable when
they did get to Grandma's.

Lisa, a three-year-old in a day care center, learned at an
early age that threats can boomerang, and at the same time
gave her teachers a clear picture of the way her mother handled
frustration.

"I'll be the mother and you be my kids," she announced to
her friends, and immediately, adopting a strident nagging tone,
she shouted, "It's bedtime! Get up those stairs to bed!"

Her playmates stood and looked at her, making no move to
walk in the direction she was pointing.

"I said go to bed!" she berated them, hands on hips and eyes
flashing. "I'll give you until I count ten to get up those stairs.
One! Two! Three! Four!" When she reached twelve and no one
had moved, she hesitated a moment and then, clapping her
hands over her ears, she screamed, "Oh, God, Oh, God! That
baby is crying again!"

Kathy, a fourth grade teacher, issued a threat and was
caught in a trap of her own making.

"When I *do* it — you *say* it!" she shouted.

As she stood, red-faced and angry, looking into the grinning
faces of her class, she heard her own words echoing in her mind.
Like a pricked balloon the tension which had been gradually
building throughout the morning was dissolved in a burst of
hilarious laughter.

If Kathy had said, as she meant to, "When I say it, you do

it!" she would have been implying a threat. Hanging in the air in a statement like that is an implied "or else!" Sue Spayth Riley makes the point in her book, "How to Generate Values in Young Children" that when an adult gives an "or else" she is putting the child in the position of making a choice.

An attorney noted for his ability to select a jury through skillful cross examination, was not quite as clever when it came to second-guessing his seven-year-old daughter.

"What are you doing with that hose?" he shouted angrily as he drove into the yard in time to see Paula direct a stream from the garden hose toward her brother. "How many times do I have to tell you that the hose is not a toy?"

With an impish grin, Paula turned toward her father.

"Don't you dare turn that hose on me!" he bellowed, thus offering a choice; the threat became a suggestion.

Paula thought quickly, "Would it be worth it to see her father drenched — and take the punishment that would be sure to follow?"

Her decision was to have her fun and take the consequences and as she related her story years later, she chuckled at the memory of her father standing in shocked amazement with water streaming from his pin-striped suit!

Ann, the director of a day care center told this story. "Last Friday was the pits! It had rained for two days; the cook called in sick at the last moment; I had three substitutes on the floor and when I called Mrs. Fraser to tell her Sammy had an earache, she didn't come for him for three hours. I let myself get drawn into a hassle with one of the kids who goes to public kindergarten in the morning and comes to us in the afternoon. He deliberately threw some paint at Harvey Jackson but instead of hitting Harvey it spattered all over the wall. I told him to clean it up — and he looked right at me and said, "I won't and you can't make me! Harvey started the fight — make him clean it up!"

"I'll admit I felt like swatting him, but of course I couldn't. My next thought was, he's right! I can't make him do it. He's a big strong kid and I'm not going to get into a tussle with him. What CAN I do? To buy myself some time I stooped down so we were face to face, held him firmly by the shoulders, and looked him right in the eyes. He was surprised — waiting to see what I was going to do to him. I still didn't know — so I took my time —

and then a funny thing happened. It seemed so ridiculous—the two of us staring at each other—that the corners of my mouth began to twitch. He grinned just a little bit—still not sure of what was going on—and in another second we both burst out laughing."

The tension was broken. I said, "O.K., I didn't see what happened. I don't know who was to blame. You go get a pan of water and some sponges and I will help you clean up."

"I'll help too," Harvey chimed in, and the two of them cleaned it up—buddies again. The day was saved!

What can you do when you get yourself out on a limb? It doesn't help to change the subject, as Lisa did, but it is risky to get your back up and challenge the child to call your bluff. Paula's father learned to his sorrow that the simplest solution is to resurrect your sense of humor and try to change a crisis into a good laugh!

If there is nothing humorous about the situation, retract! At once! The longer you wait, the harder it will be.

Kathy did this, and taught her students a valuable lesson at the same time, when she said, "Well, even if I hadn't said that backwards, it would have been a dumb thing to say. You see, I was angry, and even grownups, when they are angry, say things they don't really mean. My mistake was so silly we couldn't do anything but laugh, but it isn't always that easy. Sometimes it takes courage to say 'I was wrong'."

Offering Choices When There Are No Choices

Closely related to threatening is the error of offering choices when we have already predetermined the answer.

The teacher asks sweetly, "Would you like to hear a story?" and is left in a quandary when she receives a chorus of 'no's.' Since it was her intent to have everyone sit down in one place and listen she could have said as she spread a blanket on the floor, "Now we will *all* sit right here on this story carpet and I will read to you from this new book."

"Do you want to go shopping with me?" mother asks, when

she knows there is no alternative — since she has no intention of leaving seven-year-old Andy alone. Instead she might say:

"We will be going shopping in half an hour, Andy. I need you to help me with the bundles. If we get through in time we'll stop and pick up that special glue you wanted for your model." But it should be very clear that she was not offering a choice.

On the other hand, decision making is an important part of growing up and we need to give our children many opportunities to practice. There are not many legitimate choices for very young children but with a little thought we can create them.

"Do you want the plaid skirt or the green slacks?"

"Will you have pears or sliced peaches?"

"Which crayon will you choose for your picture?"

"Do you want to hear my story or will you sit down over at the table and do some pasting and cutting?"

"Do you want to watch Sesame Street or help me make the dessert?"

At the same time it is the responsibility of the adult to set some very firm limits. "You may do this or this but you cannot do that. This time *I* will decide. Each year that you are older you will be able to make more choices. Some day you will be making all of the decisions, but you need to have lots of practice first."

One step toward that is for the child to acknowledge that a mistake has been made and that the alternative choice would have been wiser.

Eight-year-old Sam was given a choice between using his birthday money to go to the circus or buying a toy that had been touted on TV. He chose the toy, which turned out to be shoddy and broke the first day. Sam said sadly, "I didn't make a very good choice, Dad, did I?"

"I guess you're right," his father replied. "Your birthday money is gone, but I am proud that you were able to see your mistake and admit it. Now, how about letting *me* take you to the circus?"

"If it is a party, I really think you should wear a dress," Sarah's mother said. "Oh, mother, you just don't know!" was the

indignant reply. "Of course, jeans are O.K." Crestfallen, she
admitted later that she had made a poor choice. "I really wanted
to come home—everyone had on their best party clothes, but I
remembered what you said about living with bad choices!"

My own mother helped me learn a lesson when I was
thirteen that stuck with me through a whole lifetime of choice
making. We were shopping for a new winter coat—and I was
enamored of one which was shoddily made, much too sophis-
ticated, and trimmed with fake fur. She warned me that this coat
would probably have to do me for two seasons—but I held out
for my choice—and she let me make the mistake. The first time
I wore it a classmate fingered the collar and said in a snide tone,
"Is that cotton?" For most of that year I squeezed into my old
coat which was too small, or shivered in a spring coat over two
sweaters. Fortunately, I grew fast that year—and was spared
the ignominy of wearing that monstrosity for two seasons.

The "Put Down" Destroys the "I AM"

Art Linkletter wrote a book called "Children Say the
Darndest Things!" I wish someone would write another entitled
"Grownups Say the Meanest Things!"

Many adults blunder along with very little consideration of
the feelings of the children they criticize.

If we want our children to grow into self confident people
who are capable of making decisions we need to guard against
the careless words or thoughtless acts which leave permanent
scars on fragile egos. Many of us, if we can bear to admit it,
suffered through at least one such incident in our developing
years.

Johanna was an excellent kindergarten teacher. "I don't
know how she does it," the student teacher exclaimed. "I have
never seen anyone who talked so little and yet I learned so much
in her classroom. The children like and respect her. They all
seem to know just what is expected of them, and go happily
about their business without anyone standing around telling
them what to do. Her program is terrific—there is so much good
learning taking place all of the time!"

"Yes, but have you noticed how she freezes when a visitor

comes into the room?" a second teacher asked. "She seems to drop a mask over her face that is nothing like the way she looks when she is alone with the children. Some of the parents complain about her — they think she must be too cross, but they never see her the way she really is."

When her director, thinking to help Johanna raise her self image, asked her to make a brief presentation of her program at a parent meeting, she was met with an emphatic refusal.

"I can't do it!" she said, with a look of desperation. "Please don't ask me to. I will literally be sick!" Then she broke down and related an incident which had occurred when she was in the sixth grade.

"I was always shy," she said, "so when the teacher told me to stand before the class and give a three minute speech on any subject — right off the top of my head — I was terrified. After I had stumbled and mumbled through it she proceeded to ridicule me. She didn't restrict her comments to my performance — she made fun of my appearance, my posture and my stuttering. I was devastated and as a result, my lips were sealed for life. I have never been able to speak to adults since. It affected my grades through school and college because I just couldn't speak up and participate. If I was called upon in class I went through agony!"

I could understand what had happened to this teacher because I had a similar experience at about the same age. The socially acceptable routine in the small New England town where I grew up was to attend the Thursday afternoon dancing class. It was the highlight of the week for me. I wore a party dress to school that afternoon and carried my dancing slippers in a cloth bag, and when school was over I met my friends, also curled, sashed and beribboned at the Oddfellows Hall where the class was conducted. There we changed into ballet slippers, laced around our ankles, self-consciously pretending to ignore the boys, who stood with clean faces, hair neatly combed and attired in their Sunday knicker suits.

Proud mothers lined the sides of the hall, gossiping, and secretly comparing their own offspring with the rest. The first thing we did was to march around the hall, pausing in front of Miss Fern, our teacher, for a greeting. The little girls learned how to curtsy — the boys to shake hands. I had a secret crush on

Fern; I can see her now! She had curly hair and shiny brown eyes, and she always wore a white silk blouse with a short, pleated black skirt. I adored her—until one day, as we were learning the intricacies of a grand march, she called across the floor in a sharp tone, "Grace! You are out of step again! Don't you know which is your left foot?!" Somehow I managed to get through that day—but no amount of perusasion could make me go back—and I couldn't even make myself tell my mother why. I'm sure Fern didn't know that her callous treatment had left such an impression but to this day I can't quite forgive her for the wound she inflicted. In time it was covered with scar tissue, but the pain remained. All through high school and college I agonized over proms and dances, which should have left happy memories. I could dance up a storm in my own room—but when I reached the dance floor, suddenly I had two left feet!

More pathetic was Abner, a below average child between two brothers who had all the advantages of good looks, brains, and athletic prowess. Abner's father was a blue collar worker who frequently bemoaned the fact that he hadn't been able to go to college. It is possible that he saw his son as a defective copy of his own image, but for whatever reason he carped at Abner constantly. "Stupid! Dummy! Why can't you bring home good report cards like your brothers! You could do it if you would try harder!"

When the boys were in their teens, Abner's father died quite suddenly. His sons stood by their mother throughout the funeral services accepting condolences. Abner's true feelings came out when they returned from the graveside. With a sigh of relief, he sank into a comfortable chair and said, "Never again as long as I live am I going to be stupid!"

Comparison and Competition

Another common mistake made by adults is to pit one child against another, forgetting that each one is unique, and progresses at his own rate.

Sometimes parents think the way to motivate their children to greater effort is to sing the praises of one when talking to the other. Stan and Ken were married adults with children of their own before they made the discovery that their well-intentioned father had almost succeeded in making them despise each other. Over a few beers they began to speak freely.

"What always gripes me," Stan said, "is that when Dad comes to visit us he spends the whole time telling us how successful you are, how big your house is, how smart your kids are. By the time he leaves I feel like nothing."

Ken stared at him incredulously! "But that's exactly what he does to me!" he responded. "I grew up with the idea that I could never measure up to you in his estimation! I remember once when I told him about a promotion, instead of congratulating me, he went right into a story about your new office and the bonus you got!"

When you constantly compare one child with another, you succeed in making him feel inadequate, destroy his "I AM" and put his "I CAN" into reverse!

"Come out in the yard when you finish supper," Billy's father said. "I'm going to teach you how to stand up and hit that baseball if it takes me all night! I'm sick of having that brother of mine telling me what a great player your cousin is!" Taking time out to play ball with his son would be commendable, but in this case his motivation soured the whole experience.

"Katy Sullivan called today," mother said at the dinner table. "She pretended that she wanted a recipe, but she really wanted to tell me her Katherine brought home a report card with five A's. I wouldn't give her the satisfaction of telling her what you got, Mary, I was too ashamed. I know you are just as smart as Katherine. You just aren't trying hard enough. I think we will have to cut out all television until you can do better!"

If television was really interfering with Mary's completion of her homework, taking away some of her viewing time might have been a logical punishment. To expect her to match the performance of another was unfair. Each human being is unique, with some special inherent talents. Praise for the things she could be rightfully proud of would have enabled Mary's mother to encourage her to improve in her academic skills. Instead she probably succeeded in making her feel angry and inadequate.

"But we live in a highly competitive society!" I hear someone saying. "We must train our children to compete or they will get buried when they get out into the real world."

In this book, I am talking about children up to the age of eight—and in those years they have so much growing and learning to do that we hamper them when we lay on the extra emotional strain of competition with their peers. Better instead—encourage each child to compete against his own record. As Johnny stands up against the wall to be measured we can say, "See, this line is a whole inch higher than it was last time. Think how many more things you can do now!"

"Today you swam across the pool—next you can try to swim from one end to the other!"

Bribes and Rewards

When and how are they effective? To offer a bribe before the deed is accomplished puts a great strain on the child. "If you don't cry at the dentist's I will buy you that model airplane," adds one more burden to an already overloaded circuit. Wait until the session is over and then say, "You really were brave! I was proud of you. Let's go buy that model plane!"

Bribes are like blackmail—the demands increase until the parent is buying behavior which should be taken for granted.

On the other hand, a prize is all the sweeter when it has been honestly earned. It doesn't always have to be something to hold in your hand—a word of praise, a pat on the shoulder, or a quick hug indicates approval and builds self confidence.

Of course we all dream of showing the world a courteous, polite, well-mannered child, but let's put first things first. Is our own pride at stake? Do we want "*them*" to give us brownie credits for training our children in social graces? Or do we want to help our children apply the lubrication which will smooth their way through an aggressive, critical, and often antagonistic world? To pressure children to mouth the words "please," "thank you," "excuse me" without any comprehension of their meaning is like feeding them butter without the bread. Good manners grow out of feelings — and concern for the welfare of others. We can, however, establish a climate in our homes which is gradually absorbed. When a child asks for something, we do not have to get coy and demand the "magic word." A quiet "please" as you hand it to him — followed by "thank you" if he doesn't say it first will suffice. But when he does say it, without any prompting from you, compliment him. "You remembered to say 'please'! You are really growing up!"

Gold Stars

One form of rewarding a child for behavior which has been popular for as long as I can remember is to offer a visible reward, such as a gold star placed on a chart or stuck on the back of his hand. This method seems to work, for a while, but it is like applying a bandaid without first cleaning the wound. True discipline is not something you can paste on a child's exterior; it comes from within when he sees the point in being good and WANTS to be good.

In one sense rewarding a child with a gold star for brushing his teeth is belittling his intelligence and we all like to believe our children are smart. A few words of praise, "your teeth look shiny clean, you must have been brushing them everyday" or of appreciation "Thank you for picking up your toys so I could vacuum your rug. It was real sharp of you to remember that this was my day for cleaning" will give your child an inner glow which far surpasses the effect of the gold star.

Demanding Apologies

"You apologize to your sister right now," Mrs. Jewett screamed at her eight-year-old son, Roger. "You broke her new skateboard. Tell her you're sorry!"

Roger stood there with a mutinous expression, glaring at his sister Alice. "She left it in the way," he muttered. "Can I help it if she's stupid?"

Alice interrupted her wailing with an indignant cry. "You're a clumsy fool!" she screamed. "Why can't you look where you're going?"

"Never mind that," her mother yelled. "I said to apologize and I mean it!"

Still no answer from Roger.

"O.K. then, you're going to sit right in that chair until you apologize."

Five minutes later, realizing that he couldn't win, Roger muttered, "I'm sorry" and ran into his room, slamming the door.

Was he sorry? Of course not. What did he learn? That grownups are unfair, but because they are bigger and stronger, they hold the power. A basic lesson in the theory that "might is right."

Laura, the teacher in the day care center, felt that children should be made to apologize.

When three-year-old Therese snatched Joseph's paper and ripped it in two, Laura grabbed her by the arm.

"That was a naughty thing you did," Laura shouted,

shaking Therese roughly. "You made Joseph cry! He was going to take that paper to his mother. How many times do I have to tell you to keep your hands to yourself? Now you tell him you are sorry. Apologize to Joseph!"

The word was unfamiliar and incomprehensible to Therese, who made no attempt to comply.

Taking her into the foyer where the receptionist was working, Laura sat Therese down hard, saying in a cross tone, "Now you sit right there until you are ready to apologize," and she went back to her group. She came back several times in the next hour to say, "When you are ready to say you are sorry, you can come back with us." Therese did not respond, either with tears or anger; instead she used her own defense weapon — she messed her pants!

Later, when she was reproved for her actions, Laura was defensive. "Kids have to learn to say they are sorry — and it is our job to teach them," she insisted. "I may have been wrong to leave her there so long — but I still think she should have been made to apologize."

There are many parents — and teachers — who would agree with her. They believe that forcing children to "mouth" the words will teach them to be sorry. Actually what they learn is that when you are small it is better to do what "they" tell you to, or you will be punished. In short, they are being programmed to be hypocritical.

Therese was only three, and it was unlikely that this incident did any lasting damage, but Greg, a fifth grader, had already developed his own set of values.

"Greg is in the office," the teacher's aide reported to the fifth grade teacher. "He was very rude to me and he refused to apologize."

Before Mrs. Carter could question the young aide further, Greg came into the room. He handed her the office pass and went to his desk where he slumped into a chair, his face dark with anger.

Mrs. Carter ignored him while she gave directions to the rest of her class and then pulled a chair over and sat down beside him.

"What happened, Greg?" she asked in a low voice.

He looked up angrily. "It wasn't my fault! She started it! She told me to get in line and when I did she yelled at me for getting in the front! So I yelled back! Then she took my baseball cap and said she wouldn't give it back until I apologized! Well, I won't, because it wasn't my fault!" He ended his tirade with, "And she's not keeping my cap!"

Mrs. Carter sighed inwardly. Baseball caps were a symbol. The boys never took them off. Even the principal had given up insisting that they remove them inside the building. She knew that when Miss White took Greg's cap it was the most inflammatory action she could have taken.

"Greg," she began, "I understand that you are angry because you think Miss White was unfair. I wasn't there so I won't talk about what happened, but I *do* know this. All your life you will run into things which seem unfair and find that you can't do anything about it. The important thing for you to learn is self-control. When you lose your self-control things always get worse."

"I'm not going to apologize," repeated Greg, with no sign of weakening. "I hate her!"

"I'm sorry to hear you say that," his teacher replied. "Hate is a very wasteful emotion. It doesn't usually hurt the other person, but it acts like a poison on the one who does the hating."

Greg looked up and for the first time there was a gleam of understanding in his eye. "Well, I don't *like* her!" he said emphatically.

"Ah, now that's all right. You don't have to like everyone. You don't have to like me or Miss White, or even the principal. However, when people are in authority you do have to accept their orders, even if you disagree with them. I can understand that you really aren't sorry that you talked back to Miss White, because you meant what you said. However, you lost your self control. You should always be sorry when that happens. I wonder if you could say that to Miss White? Not that you admit that she was right but simply that you are sorry you lost your self control and spoke rudely."

"No," said Greg, but his voice had lost some of its assurance.

"Think about it," Mrs. Carter said, as she pushed back her chair. "This can build up, with the principal involved, and maybe your mother, or it can all be settled in a couple of minutes" and she walked away.

Half an hour later, when the school day ended, Greg said to Miss White, "I'm sorry I was rude" and received his cap.

But Mrs. Carter's task was only half done. She still had to talk to the young aide.

"I want to remind you," she began, "that Greg was transferred to this school only a few weeks ago because he had become such a problem, and the authorities thought a change of scene might help. We were warned that he was a headstrong child with an explosive temper. He has been doing very well but you came close to setting off a catastrophe today."

Miss White's lips were tight in a scowling face. "I'm not letting any fifth grader talk back to me!" she stated flatly.

"I'm not suggesting that you do," Mrs. Carter said, "but I do believe that you might have handled things differently to begin with, or, once having reached an impasse, that it was up to you to find a better solution. Taking Greg's cap was unwise, and unfair. Demanding an apology was even more unwise. Expecting Greg, in the heat of his anger — and he certainly felt it was righteous anger — to admit that he was wrong was asking the impossible of him at that moment."

"But he did apologize!" Miss White pointed out with an air of triumph.

"No," Mrs. Carter shook her head. "He is a bright child. I was able to make him see the difference between being wrong, and being out of control, or as he would say 'losing his cool.' Greg told you he was sorry he was rude and even that took a big effort on his part. I was able to help him *see the sense in acting in a certain way*' which is what self discipline is all about. I think you need to accept that, and reflect on other ways that you might have managed this whole episode."

Requiring a child to apologize is a sensitive issue which I have heard debated heatedly at both parent and teachers' meetings. There will probably be many who read this who truly believe that it is right to insist that children utter the correct words, even though they are directly opposed to their true feelings. If we are really concerned with helping them we will seek other avenues as Mrs. Carter did.

Nagging and Scolding

The last, and most common of the deadly sins is that we *all talk too much*!

"How many times do I have to tell you...."

"If I've told you once I've told you a hundred times...."

"I'm not going to tell you once more...."

"And I mean it!"

Does that sound familiar? Do you wonder that our children learn at an early age to tune us out? Our very words contradict our actions, like the teacher who stands before her class, screaming Q-U-I-E-T!!!

I listened to a teacher in a child care center carrying on a continuous monologue.

"Johnny put your rubbers on." "Get your rubbers on, Johnny." "Have your got your rubbers yet, Johnny?"

She went on and on—like water dripping out of a leaky faucet—repeating the same words. If she had listened to a tape recording of her performance she probably would have been amazed. Why hadn't she just walked over to Johnny—handed him his rubbers and encouraged or helped him to put them on? She used up so much of her precious energy with useless "yakking" that it was not surprising that she was exhausted at the end of the day.

There is only a slight difference between this meaningless patter and nagging.

"Have you done your homework?"

"Be sure to hang up your coat."

"Put those toys away, remember your father fell over them last week!"

"Wash your hands."

"You tracked mud on my clean floor!"

"Stop teasing your sister."

This slides naturally into self pity.

"I worked so hard to get that nice jacket for you and now you tell me you left it on the playground!"

"I spent all afternoon fixing you a nice dinner and now you don't even finish it!"

Marcus spent his early years in an orphanage. He was proud that he had been able to provide his children with a good home—and wanted to make certain that they appreciated it. He made a point of talking about the food on the table, reminding them that he knew what it was to be hungry. He also wanted them to appreciate their mother and insisted that each child say 'thank you' to her at the conclusion of every meal. Marcia, his wife, was amused and surprised when her four-year-old son reacted in an unexpected fashion. On one of their shopping trips he had gone into a mild tantrum when she refused to buy the sugar coated cereal he wanted. When he ran away from her she calmly ignored him until she heard him shout from the other side of the market, "And anyway I hate your cookin'!"

But of all the useless verbal exercise in parent-child communications probably the saddest is the parent who is afraid to say "no"; who engages in lengthy arguments with her children, listening with far too much patience while they rationalize, explain, complain, delay, stall and manipulate her until they win the advantage. Children *do not want* to run the show. They have a right to expect that adults will set some limits and maintain control. It gives them a comfortable feeling of security to know that "they won't let me." It is my opinion that when parents abdicate this responsibility their behavior borders on cruel and abusive!

CHAPTER 11

Call in the Reserves

Sometimes a disciplinary situation can get so out of hand that the parties involved need the advice of an outside observer — one who can stand to one side and view the problem in an unemotional way. Joan, recently appointed director of the day care center where she had been a teacher, found herself floundering in deep water, and was wise enough to call on her supervisor for help. On the day that Liz arrived she saw two lively little boys clambering over the furniture in the front office where a tight-lipped secretary was trying to work.

"Why are those children in here on this beautiful afternoon?" she asked.

"*She* sent them in!" was the muttered answer. "They spend more time in here with me than they do in the classroom. I don't know how they can expect me to get my work done if I have to play baby sitter to a couple of little devils. What am I supposed to say if a parent walks in and asks me what they are doing?" Glaring at the boys she hollered, "Sit down, you kids, and don't get off that bench until I tell you to!"

"I'll take care of them," Liz said quietly, and taking each of the boys by the hand she calmly walked away. "It's such a nice day I think you need to be outside," she said, as she took them back to their teacher who was on the playground.

Later when Liz and Joan, the center director, were in the office Joan brought up the incident. "I know you were upset because those boys were inside," she began, "but they have pushed us all beyond the limits of our patience."

"Let's talk about them," Liz replied. "How many hours do they spend here?"

"Better than fifty hours a week. They are the first to arrive in the morning—and usually the last to leave. Their parents work in town, and car pool, so they come together."

"They seem to be bright," Liz said. "Some of their antics and the language that accompanied it were highly imaginative."

"Oh, they are bright all right," Joan exclaimed. "What one doesn't think of, the other will. They egg each other on and get into all kinds of mischief."

"How do they get along with the other children?" was Liz's next question.

"That's part of the problem; they are very popular. The other children admire them and copy their behavior."

"What have you done about it?" Liz queried.

"Well, I've asked their parents to talk to them, but that hasn't seemed to do any good. I think I'll have to tell them tonight that if these boys can't behave, I can't keep them. They are wearing out the staff. What do *you* think I ought to do?"

"I'm glad you asked," Liz laughed. "But first, let me tell you one of my favorite stories."

Mrs. and Mrs. Herbert Jones had just boarded the train from London for their annual summer holiday at the coast. Mr. Jones immediately settled back with his paper, leaving his harried wife to manage the two children, ages three and four. As the journey progressed, their behavior grew worse. Mrs. Jones finally turned to her husband, nudging him angrily, and said, "That son of yours is behaving like a brat. Speak to him!"

Lowering his paper, Mr. Jones said in a mild tone, "Ello, Erbie" and went back to reading his paper.

Ignoring Joan's weak attempt at a smile, Liz went on. "I'm afraid that asking these parents to 'speak to' their children would be as ineffective as Erbie's father's response. Have you thought about how they feel? Try to imagine what they must be saying to each other as they fight the traffic after working hard all day."

"I wonder if she's going to greet me again with a laundry list of all the bad things Rick has done today."

"Yeah, I can tell the minute I see her face if they have been bad."

"My kid is no angel, but he's not really bad. I'm paying good money. If these teachers were doing their job, there wouldn't be a problem."

"What if she won't keep them? The boss will never give me time off again to go looking for another center—and besides I hate to admit that my four-year-old son has been expelled."

Joan looked chagrined. "I guess I have been thinking only of our side," she admitted.

"There's something else," Liz went on, "What do you think happens when they leave here after you have burned their parent's ears with your complaints? Can't you hear them scolding and threatening all the way home? Good day care should support and strengthen parent-child relationships—not destroy them!

"Now let's think of some actions you *can* take. First, instead of greeting their parents with stories of their misdemeanors I want you to have at least one positive thing to tell them every single night for the next week. No matter how devilish the children may have been during the day, keep it to yourself!"

"What if there isn't anything good to say?" protested Joan.

"That will be your challenge. If you really observe them, you will find something. Maybe it will be helping another child. Or putting away something without being told. Or being the first to come when their group is called. Or making a great building in the block center. It doesn't have to be a dramatic incident. If it is positive, the parents will probably enlarge it in their minds anyway. At this point, I expect they are grasping at straws."

"I want you to share this directive with the rest of the staff. They, too, are to look for something good instead of reinforcing the negative by complaining to each other. If you all concentrate on looking for good things to report I am sure that you will see definite improvement in the children. Just lifting the burden of guilt from the parents' shoulders by not complaining to them every night is bound to help, too. I will call you in a week, and if you are still having trouble, we may want to ask the parents to come in for a conference. If you like, I will come out and sit in on it with you.

"Another thing—look through those books on your shelf and find some literature that tells what four-year-olds are like. Give it to your staff to review—and then plan a staff meeting around Ages and Stages. At the same time, take a good look at your program to see how well it is meeting the needs of these bright, active boys. Can it be they are bored?

"Finally, ask your lead teacher to keep a diary on both children. Record every incident—noting the time of day, people involved, what was done about it, and their reactions. We may see some kind of pattern emerge which will help us to work out a solution. If we are going to be responsible for such a large part of their waking hours, we must try very hard to improve on the quality of that time. I particularly want to see what activity they gravitate toward most often. We need to capitalize on their special interests. Perhaps you can give them more of it—or at least try not to take them away when they are truly involved.

"When you have established a better rapport with the parents, you may be able to help them with suggestions for things which they can do at home, based on your knowledge of four-year-olds."

Keeping her word, Liz called Joan one week later.

"How are you getting along with your problem children?" she asked.

"What problem children?" was the cheery response. "We can't believe that there could be so much change in just one week! Your suggestions were so simple—but they worked!"

Teachers and Parents Understand Each Other

— This is an example of the need for parents and teachers to establish a sympathetic, understanding relationship. Joan was piling unnecessary pressures on the shoulders of harried parents who were already feeling guilty. They, in turn, were scolding and punishing their children when they should have been enjoying them in the limited time they shared.

Don't Try to "Wing It" Alone

The responsibility for a growing child is too great to be borne by a single individual. There are reserve sources available to everyone—but most of us are reluctant to seek their advice because we see it as an admission of our own inadequacies. If we are lucky there are grandmothers waiting to be asked, hesitating for fear they will be accused of interfering. Relatives, friends, neighbors, somewhere among them there is a kindly soul who would be glad to serve as your sounding board.

Young single parents who are working and trying to be good parents at the same time feel very lonely. They are usually short on social life and exhausted because their physical and emotional energy is stretched thin. A truly committed day care director is always ready to lend a listening ear or a comforting shoulder, because she knows it is the child who will ultimately benefit.

Teachers also fail to call upon resources their colleagues and superiors can offer, and for the same reason. My advice to them is that it is a mistake to try to "wing it" alone when there are people who have been where you are and who would be happy to give you the benefit of their experience. Your principal or supervisor will not think less of you for admitting that you have a lot to learn, and everyone likes to be asked for advice!

Who are *your* reserves? Look around you; they are there!

CHAPTER **12**

Some Thoughts on Punishment

With our eyes still focused on *"helping children to see the sense in acting in a certain way"* we will now explore the place of punishment in discipline.

First we need a guideline for determining when punishment is legitimate. In my opinion this is one area which can be as clearly defined as if there were a black line drawn right down the middle of the page.

When the behavior of an individual infringes on the rights of another person, it is a misdemeanor. This boils down to "You may not hurt people," and "You may not destroy property." I would add for good measure "You may not be rude or fresh to adults."

What are Your "Or Elses"?

Punishment implies consequences. In simplified terms I talk about "or elses." Just as the adult who breaks the law knows that if he is caught he will be fined, or if the crime is serious enough, he may go to jail, so the child needs to know that something unpleasant *will* happen if he breaks a rule. Unfortunately, in the adult world there are many inconsistencies, loopholes, ways which permit the culprit to avoid unhappy consequences. Since Watergate there has been a trend toward exposing those who flagrantly break the laws of our country. Through the media we have been alternately angry and sympathetic toward public officials, politicians, lawyers and law

makers who have, in some cases been shocked to find themselves
in jail! Our children must have a hard time understanding why
it is important for them to obey the basic rules of society!

What are the most commonly used "or elses" for children
under eight years of age? They usually fall into three categories:
spanking, isolation, and withdrawal of privileges.

Spanking

"I have just as much right to hit you as you have to hit me!"
Douglas shouted as he kicked his father in the most sensitive
area of his leg — the shin bone.

Frank Farrar drew back in surprise and anger. His first
reaction was to reach for his five-year-old-son and let him know
who was boss, but the ridiculousness of the situation struck him.
Here he was, a six foot, one hundred and ninety pound man
standing off against a five-year-old-boy who tipped the scales at
forty-five, soaking wet. He gave himself a second to cool down
and then said calmly, "You have a point there, son. It was wrong
of you to kick me; it hurts like the devil, and it was also wrong of
me to whack you. I expect that hurt too. Striking out is not the
best way to settle a problem. Let's talk about it and see if we
can't figure out a better way. You had no business using my
tools without permission and now you have spoiled an expensive
saw. What do you think would be a fair punishment for what you
did?"

Frank had come into my kitchen to solicit funds for the
March of Dimes and found me sitting dejectedly at the kitchen
table. I had just administered an over-the-knee walloping to my
six-year-old-son, and I was still flushed with anger and exertion.

"Sure, I'll make a contribution," I wailed, "but I feel like a
hypocrite. I can give money to help other kids, but I can't
manage my own son without beating up on him. There must be a
better way!"

"I know just how you feel," Frank said sympathetically, and
told me his story.

"I have to admit I was kind of proud of Douglas for having the guts to stand up to me," he said, "and it made me think about *why* I spanked him. I realized that it was usually to relieve *my* feelings. I might have used the old cliché 'I'm doing this for your own good,' or 'this hurts me more than it hurts you' but it wasn't true and he was smart enough to know it! My father always took his belt to me and I was just carrying on the pattern! I decided then that I had to find other ways to handle discipline. I figured that if Douglas was smart enough to know that spanking didn't make any sense I could try talking to him as an intelligent human being."

Spanking is a very controversial subject. It is almost invariably brought up at every parent meeting or discipline workshop. On a smaller scale and at a different level it is like the on-going discussion of capital punishment. There will always be arguments on both sides, and in the case of spanking the balance is usually tipped in favor of it as a legitimate form of punishment. The proponents will say:

"The flat of the hand applied on a child's bottom has a dramatic effect. It says more clearly than words, 'O.K., you have stepped over the boundaries, and this is the consequence.' It relieves my feelings and lets my kid know I'm mad. A good spanking clears the air!"

William, aged three, wasn't ready to accept that notion. His parents were deeply involved in a political campaign just prior to a national election. It was Sunday, a day when William's father ordinarily spent time playing and talking with his son. Both parents had been busy all day on the phone and with paper work and William was expressing his annoyance with their preoccupation.

"You said you would play ball with me! You're mean — and I hate you!" he shouted and at the same time pushed a pile of papers off the table onto the floor. Whereupon his father spanked him and sent him to his room. In a few minutes he said, "O.K., you can come out now!" but William chose to remain in his room and sulk. When he was called for dinner, he refused to answer. Going to the door his father said in a kindly tone, "All right, son, that's enough! You were a fresh kid and you deserved that spanking, but it's over. Now lets forget it — come eat your dinner!"

"Well, you didn't have to hit me!" William retorted. "And anyhow I am going to vote for Nixon!" Having had the last word he came to the table and the incident was closed.

Six-year-old Jerry viewed spanking from a different perspective.

"You don't love me as much as Jeannie!" he complained to his mother when she was tucking him in at bedtime.

"Why, Jerry, how can you say such a thing?" she replied in astonishment. "Of course I love you both the same!"

"But you spank her—and you never spank me," was his wistful answer.

Jerry was hit by a truck when the twins were four years old. For a time his life hung in the balance, and when he did recover he was left with some minimal brain damage and a permanently crippled leg. Because she had come so close to losing him, his mother had never been able to bring herself to punish him, and he evidently interpreted this as a lack of affection. His perceptive comment made her rethink her attitudes. She had been quick to insist that he be treated like everyone else—but she hadn't been following her own rules. His unexpected reaction was an example of the insight and wisdom children will demonstrate if we take time to listen to their thoughts.

When we set reasonable limits for our children and punish them for their transgressions we convey a message of love. Jerry needed that wonderful secure feeling of knowing that his mother cared for him too much to let his behavior get out of bounds.

The whole subject of spanking touches on a tender nerve because I spanked my own children, but if I could have a second chance, knowing what I do today, I would *not* ever lay a hand on them in punishment! To begin with I would see it as an admission of failure. Child rearing is a constant challenge. I know now that each behavioral problem has a solution—and spanking is the easy way out. If I had been exposed to the four steps: **ANTICIPATE! HESITATE! INVESTIGATE!** and **COMMUNICATE!** I think I could have been more imaginative in solving the problems.

A friend once said to me, "No two children in the same family have the same two parents!" At first that seemed like a ridiculous statement, but as I thought about it I realized that with each succeeding child we do change in our attitudes and maturity. The first child is often the victim of the fumbling and bumbling of inexperience!

Almost from the day my first son was born he had me bewildered and buffaloed. From the very beginning he wore a strong will like an armored breastplate, and at a very early age his vivid imagination led him into some weird adventures! I didn't understand him, and I didn't know how to cope with him, so I spanked...and spanked...and spanked! When he was four, I was the teacher in a small private nursery school. The story which follows sent my mind racing back to those days when I was so afraid someone would think I was favoring my own child over the others that I was actually cruel to him.

Wearing Two Hats!

When Judy saw Mrs. Baker, the center director, approaching with a visiting mother and her child, she glanced apprehensively at her own daughter, Amanda, who was playing happily in the housekeeping corner with two friends.

"Mrs. Easton and Sarah would like to stay awhile," Mrs. Baker said. "Perhaps Sarah can play with the toys while you tell her mother about your program."

Just then Amanda looked up and saw the visitors. Her face clouded over, and within a few seconds there was an outburst from that part of the room. Amanda was holding tightly to Louisa's doll, while Louisa, crying loudly, tried to retrieve it. Amanda was grinning, obviously enjoying her playmate's unhappiness.

"Amanda! Give that doll right back!" Judy admonished in a harsh tone. "You know better than to tease poor Louisa! She had it first!"

Now it was Amanda's turn to burst into tears. She flung herself at her mother but Judy pushed her away continuing in an angry voice, "Stop acting like a baby and go play. You can see that I am busy!"

"You always blame me! It wasn't my fault! She called me a bad name!" Amanda whined. Turning away she went over to a table where four children were working and tried to pull up a chair and sit down.

"You can't sit here!" they said. "You know only four people can sit at this table at the same time!"

Amanda ran back to her mother, crying again. "They won't let me play with them!" she complained.

"Well, you knew better than to try to sit there," Judy answered, crossly. "Now go find something to do. I need to talk to this lady. This is her little girl, Sarah. Sarah might want to come here to school. Why don't you help her find some toys?"

Amanda's answer was to try to crawl into her mother's lap. Judy pushed her away. "Not now, Amanda," she said, more gently. "When we go home you can sit in my lap."

Amanda dragged over a chair and sat as close to Judy as she could. Judy tried to ignore her. Failing to get her attention, Amanda put her hands into her mother's smock pockets. When this didn't work, she began to make small annoying noises.

"It's very hard to have your own child in your class," Judy commented with an apologetic smile.

"I can see that," Mrs. Easton replied. "I think it must be very hard on a child to have to share her mother with so many other children!"

When Judy had a break later that day she headed for the director's office. "I have come to give my notice," she announced, her lips quivering. "I love my job but Amanda is driving me up a wall. How is it that I can be so patient and understanding with all of the other children and unable to cope with my own? Mrs. Easton will never want to send Sarah here after what happened this morning. It was awful."

"Yes, she told me about it," Mrs. Baker replied. "I think she could see what was going on, and apparently she was sympathetic to your problem because she did enroll Sarah. Let's talk about it. I don't want to lose you!"

"And I don't want to go," Judy said emphatically, "but Amanda has to come first, and she is having a hard time. It is affecting her at home, too. She whines a lot, and a couple of times lately she wet her bed. She stopped that over a year ago!"

"I regret that we didn't talk about this when I hired you," Mrs. Baker went on. "I have seen it happen before, and if we had tried to **ANTICIPATE** it we might have saved you both some heartaches."

The bond between a mother and her child is almost like a

permanent umbilical cord. You must try to understand how Amanda feels when she suddenly has to share *her* mother with a whole roomful of children. She hasn't had the time to develop much emotional strength, and when you push her away how can she be sure that you aren't forsaking her? It hurts!"

"I know you are right," Judy answered, "and I hate myself for it. I can't go on doing that to my child! The sad part is that Amanda really loves school and she needs the companionship. There is no one in our neighborhood for her to play with.

"My problem is that I am so afraid I will favor her that I lean too far the other way. I don't want the other children, or their parents, or even the other teachers to think that I am giving her special privileges, so I never let her be the one to go first, or give the answers, or talk when we have a meeting. I expect her to share, even when she brings something from home. I'm really mean to her! Perhaps I can leave and get a job somewhere else so I can afford to keep on sending her here!"

"There are a few things we can try before you do anything drastic about leaving," replied Mrs. Baker. "When the children are napping, come back and I will make some suggestions."

Later, when they were able to talk without interruption, Mrs. Baker said, "I should have warned you to talk with Amanda about your new job before you ever came to work. You could have said something like 'When we go to school, I will be a teacher and I will have to take care of lots of children, but I will still be your Mummy, and you will be the *only* one who is *my little girl.*' It would be a mistake to expect her to fully understand what this will mean, but the idea will have been planted, and you can talk more about it when she is faced with sharing your attention. Without the benefit of that advance preparation, let's think of what you can do to handle it now. When she does make demands, I urge you to put up with it. I know it is irritating when she clings to you, cries and whines a lot and wants to sit on your lap. I can understand your frustration when she interrupts and makes a scene because you are paying attention to another child, but it will come out better in the long run if you grin and bear it. Do not scold her or push her away. Try to remember that she is really hurting, and that your rejection is like rubbing salt in the wound. I promise you that it will not last forever! As soon as she is really convinced that she comes first in your affection she will not need to test you, and she will be able to get on with the business of play without keeping one eye on you.

"You say that you are afraid that *they* will think you are favoring your own child. Who are *they*? The other teachers? I will talk about this at a staff meeting, and I am sure you will find them sympathetic. Some of them have been through it! Are you worried about the other parents? As long as *you* know that you are being completely fair and that you are not giving Amanda special privileges, you need not be concerned. They are more likely to judge your teaching skills by the way you interact with your own child."

As more and more mothers are looking for part-time jobs to supplement the family income, work in a child care center has many attractive features. Having your own child accompany you eliminates the problem and expense of making outside arrangements, and the hours can often be matched to the school attendance of other children in the family. In fact, some mothers will take the job, as Judy did, primarily to be able to give their own children the benefit of a good nursery school or kindergarten experience.

When my first child was four years old, I took him with me to nursery school and I made this mistake. I was so afraid that the other mothers would resent him that I was downright mean! The more I pushed him away, the more he demanded attention with unruly behavior. We were both miserable by the time we walked home at noon. Every day, he ran ahead of me so he could get the hairbrush and hide it! We laugh when this story is told now at family gatherings, but I still harbor feelings of shame and regret! However, he saw to it that I paid my dues!

After his first year of college, he decided to go into naval officer training. When he came home at the end of three months, I met him in the airport, and my heart swelled with pride. The shaggy haired, sloppily dressed boy who had left home had returned a MAN, trim and handsome in his navy uniform with gold braid! When I ran to embrace him he held me close, and affectionately gave me several not so gentle spanks. That pattern was repeated every time we were reunited after an absence, and although they were ostensibly love pats they hurt! They stopped as suddenly as they had begun, and to this day I am not sure whether he was expressing affection or paying me back, spank for spank! Could there have been some kind of a computer in his memory which recorded the exact number?

When parents who advocate spanking say "I am doing this for your own good!" or "It hurts me more than it does you!" do such statements belittle the intelligence of the child? Will hitting really teach them to mend their ways? Or will it leave them with the sure knowledge that the world belongs to the strong?

There is a distinction between spanking and a "back of the woodshed over the knee" walloping. If I had to take a stand on the subject, I would at least eliminate the use of anything other than the flat of the hand. Using a switch, ruler, hairbrush, stick or belt is dangerous. In many cases, the person who needs to punish a child in this way is not able to control his own emotions, and it is too easy to cross over the line from punishment to abuse.

To conclude this subject I am reminded of a friend who brought up three lively boys. "I kept a stick by the door," she said. "One day when I came into the kitchen and found them spraying each other with ketchup I grabbed the stick and hit the nearest chair with a mighty crack. You would think I had hit one of them! They looked at me with startled expressions, and started in meekly to clean up the mess. After that, she chuckled, my stick had a way of disappearing, until they got a little older and realized that I was all noise and no action!"

Isolation and Separation

Fortunately physical punishment is now banned in schools in nearly all states and the method I saw used most frequently was isolation. Since the child who is acting up is usually demanding attention, it seems logical to remove him from the scene. It is the way that separation is handled that is important. In the home a parent can send the child to his room; the teacher does not have that luxury, and some of the alternatives I have witnessed make me uncomfortable. I would strongly urge a parent who is investigating child care to ask the director how she handles discipline.

The "Thinking Chair"

A very common practice is the "thinking chair" or some adaptation of it. In my opinion this is a close cousin to the dunce's stool used by our forefathers. I have vivid memories of children in child care centers of every description, sitting on a chair set apart from the group. Some of them were showing off, gaining the attention they wanted. Some were bored and resigned. I ached for the little ones who were all scrunched up, sad and miserable, and I saw a few who looked like firecrackers ready to explode. When the thinking chair is used to embarrass or humiliate, it loses its purpose. When a child is told, "Sit there until you can behave," we seem to be overlooking the fact that if he *could* control himself there would be no reason to send him away. The angry child has a tremendous need to let out whatever is causing his trouble—either through words or actions. Leaving him to handle his feelings alone can only intensify the anger, fear or hurt which caused the behavior in the first place.

From a practical point of view if your purpose is to get a child away from the scene of the action it is better to take a low key approach. If you demand of a three or four year old, "Sit on that chair!" you had best have Plan B to follow if he laughs at you and runs away. Tying him down is frowned upon, and he may be a young Houdini, able to wiggle out of the most secure bonds.

Isolation is effective when the focus is on the child rather than his misdeeds. A teacher can say, "You must not be feeling very good today," or "I need you to come over here and calm down—then we can talk. This can be your own special place for a while. No one else can use it until you are through with it."

It could be a beanbag chair, a place to crawl into like a blanket over a table or a carton lined with soft pillows. In one center, I saw a child-sized waterbed where a child could relax and regain his equilibrium.

For some children separation is a real punishment. When my own children tested my endurance too far with their squabbling, I would forbid them to speak to each other for one hour by the clock. Sometimes they went their separate ways, seeking other entertainment, but more often they were pleading for a reprieve before the hour was up.

I watched a teacher in a child care center who dealt with a three year old in this way. He was amusing everyone at the lunch table by spooning his food onto the floor. She quietly took him by the hand, and set him at another table by himself. She did not berate him for his behavior, scold, or threaten him. The next day she asked, "Do you wish to eat with us today?" and when he nodded assent she made a place for him beside her and the incident was closed. Would that more teachers could talk less and *act* more!

The third commonly used method for punishing children — withdrawal of privileges — does not call for any great discussion. The main thing is to make the punishment fit the crime. Don't try to trade apples for oranges, as the saying goes. It makes sense to take away T.V. viewing time when it is apparent that is has interfered with homework. To use it as a punishment for breaking a dish or another child's toy is not appropriate. The guilty child should have to make reparations in kind. To replace an object, he could give up something of his own of like value. To make up for destroying a neighbor's flower bed, he could do some yard work.

The point is that he needs to feel the pain that his victim is experiencing.

Children can accept fair and reasonable punishment. They know when they deserve it and they feel better when they pay their dues. They are just as quick to resent unfair treatment. The teacher who keeps the whole class after school because the kid who hit her with an eraser while her back was turned won't stand up and admit it is chalking up trouble for herself. If her children lose respect for her they will team up in their efforts to bedevil her.

The father who takes it out on his family because his boss raked him over the coals will endanger the TRUST which he might desperately need in a later confrontation.

It has been suggested that helping a child to understand

and get rid of the feelings that caused him to misbehave will have more long reaching benefits than punishment. When hostility is faced, and worked off, warm positive feelings replace anger and frustration. Limits must be set on the methods used, the appropriate place and time to work out feelings and the rules which determine the need. The point to stress is that we can "be the boss of" our own emotions, as Mrs. Carruthers put it so aptly to Joseph. Feelings must not be allowed to become the tail that wags the dog!

Punishment is an ugly word! It has traditionally stood as a symbol of power! A wise parent or teacher will look for alternative ways to deal with people problems. Some of these are described in the following chapter.

CHAPTER 13

An Ounce of Prevention

If you have decided against spanking, if isolation isn't working very well, and if you are worn out with arguments about the withdrawal of privileges, what else can you do? For some answers we turn once more to our definition. It does not say to do something *to* the child but to help him understand, to make some *sense* out of the reasons for the way people behave.

The first step in bringing about that understanding is to talk openly and honestly about feelings, or emotions. It is important for the child to recognize that we all have strong feelings, both children and grownups. Everyone feels mad, and sad, and glad and that it is all right to do so. Feelings are the propelling force in the developing personality. They provide the contrast that makes life rich and meaningful. Without some grief or sadness one could never truly appreciate happiness. Peace of mind is sweeter when it follows a period of frustration and the person who has suffered loneliness and rejection can recognize and appreciate love all the more when he finds it. Our feelings can work for us or against us. If we deny them, push them down into the deep dark recesses of the subconscious, they fester and grow like a nasty virus, and sooner or later they erupt and someone gets hurt.

Good feelings need to be exposed also, talked about and demonstrated. There was a song which was popular back in the sixties—"Accentuate the Positive!" It was based on what present day educators call positive reinforcement. It is as simple as waking up on a sunny day, feeling great and saying so. It means touching, expressing affection, giving a word of praise,

117

making a positive comment about another's appearance or behavior thus giving the "I AM" a spin in the right direction.

We know that our children learn from watching the way we act, and copying the behavior of the adults they most admire. We have a choice. We can teach them to be positive or negative in their outlook.

If you start the day with a doleful "Another lousy rainy day!" your very words have the power to make the clouds darker. If, with a shrug of the shoulder and a knowing expression you intimate that you know something bad about another person, you are not only reinforcing your own derogatory thoughts but it is almost certain that someone will get the message and pass it on, and that the negative aspects will get worse with each retelling.

The power of emotion can be compared with that of the sun. Scientists are presently seeking ways to harness solar energy and put it to use. We know that the sun is potentially dangerous. A concentration of its rays on the human body can cause a painful sunburn, or when they are focused on a piece of glass they can set off a raging forest fire. In a similar way our emotions can be a destructive force if they are allowed to burst forth uncontrolled.

But the sun is also a source of warmth, light, and power. To repeat a favorite expression, when your children are allowed to "bask in the light of your approval" they will thrive and grow.

Bring the Feelings Out in the Open

Dorene, the mother of two lively little boys had learned how to help children find ways to express their feelings when she was a kindergarten teacher. Now she was hard pressed to use that experience for the benefit of Craig, her first-born. He was a very bright creative child whose mental excursions often carried him outside the boundaries of rules. He was not deliberately disobedient or inattentive, but when the wheels were turning inside his active mind he moved in a world of his own, and appeared to be a law unto himself.

In the second grade he encountered a teacher of the "old school" who was determined to squeeze this square peg into the round mold of conformity. It was a classic case of an immovable object coming up against an irresistible force. What Craig lacked in size he made up for with stubborn determination. Day after day he came home from school in a state of anger and frustration which he usually took out on his younger brother. Dorene wanted him to know that she understood his conflict, but at the same time she knew that he was the one who would have to compromise. It was obvious that his teacher was not going to give an inch.

"It's too bad that you and Mrs. Smith don't get along, she said, "but for as long as you live, there will be people who will not be willing to accept your ideas and the way you think and act. When you get a job you will have to adjust your ways to those of your boss or get fired. And if, someday, you are the boss and have people working for you, there will be times when you will have to practice patience and tolerance; so you might as well start right now. You need to find some legitimate ways to let those angry feelings which are churning around inside you escape before there is an explosion. The trick is to do it at the right time, and in the right place, so you don't hurt anyone or get yourself into more trouble."

The Pressure Cooker

Soon after that something happened which gave Dorene the perfect opportunity to demonstrate to her son what happens when feelings are kept too tightly under control. The lid of her pressure cooker blew off, hitting the ceiling, and spattering its contents all over the wall and floor.

"This is much like what happens to you on the day when Mrs. Smith has leaned on you especially hard," she said. "By the time you get home you are so filled with bad feelings that they explode, just like the pressure cooker, and anyone who gets in your way gets spattered with the hot anger that has been building up inside you."

Dictating Stories and Poems

"When you were little, before you could write, you used to let off steam by dictating stories and poems. I came across one of them the other day that you wrote when you were five. Listen to this:

'I'm mad! I'm mad! I'm mad! I am not sad!
Don't come near. Stay away!
You'd better not touch me today!
You hurt me when you squeezed my arm
Don't tell me to be calm.
You're mean! You're gruff! You think You're tough!
Don't come near
Stay away!'

"You must have been really mad when you wrote that one. I'm sure you felt better afterward. Sometimes when I get mad at your dad I write him a letter with all the angry words I feel like saying and then I put it away for a few days. When I go back and read it I usually tear it up. It's a lot better than fighting and arguing. You can't tear up or erase the mean things you say out loud. Even if you say you are sorry the hurt never quite goes away.

"When I was a kindergarten teacher, before you were born, I had a boy named Randy in my class who was giving me a lot of trouble. One day when he had me at my wits end I sat him down at a table across from me and said,

"'You are having a bad day. You hit John and now he won't play with you. You made Diane cry because you snatched the toy she brought from home and hid it. Jim and Steve chased you out of the sandbox because you smashed the castle they were building. Something must have happened to make you feel so mean. Perhaps it would help if you could talk about it, or better still, let's pretend that I am your secretary. You tell me how you feel and I will write it all down.'

He just looked at me and shook his head, but I waited.

"Why did you hit John?" I asked, thinking to get him started. That opened the flood gates. For the next five minutes I had to write very fast to keep up with him while his anger poured out.

"They all make fun of me because I wear glasses! They call me four eyes! They wouldn't let me help with their dumb castle! I can make a better castle than they can! You always hang up Diane's papers and you never hang mine! I only wanted to look at her dumb toy, but she wouldn't let me!"

On and on he sputtered. When he finally stopped I said, "Is that all?"

He looked surprised. I guess he thought I was going to scold him. "Shall I read it back to you?" I asked, "That's what a secretary would do." He nodded yes.

I wish I could have made a videotape of the expressions that crossed his face as I read his words out loud. Alternately he scowled and grinned; he frowned and beamed with approval. Little by little he relaxed.

"What shall I do with it now?" I asked him when I had finished.

"You'd better keep it. I might need it again," was his succinct reply and he went off to play.

"Did it work?" Craig asked skeptically. "Did Randy behave better after that?"

"It worked for that time," Dorene replied, "but I had to keep thinking of different ways to help him. He was having a lot of trouble getting along at home, too, and I could tell from the expression on his face when he arrived at school if we were in for a rough day."

"What other things did you do?" Craig asked, his interest now aroused.

Puppets

"Well, for one thing, I used puppets—with him and the other children. I would put one on my hand and give them the other. I gave my puppet a silly name. It was funny but the

puppets could say things to each other that the real people
couldn't.

"You like to make puppets. Perhaps you can think of a way
to use them to express your feelings."

Craig looked at Dorene thoughtfully but made no comment.
It was obvious that she had planted some ideas in his mind.

A few days later Dorene heard Craig come stamping in,
slam the door and go straight to the kitchen. This was one room
where the boys were free to use paint or clay and make a mess.
He was very quiet for a while. When she heard some sticky
plops, she went to **INVESTIGATE.** Craig had drawn a circle on
the wall with a dot in the middle. Before him was a pile of small
balls of plasticene, which he was throwing at the target. Each
time he hit a bulls eye the grin on his face suggested that the dot
was Mrs. Smith!

Many people express their anger with an instinctive reaction to throw the nearest object at hand. This isn't limited to
children, as the records in any hospital emergency ward would
show.

I remember watching the teen-aged son of the family next
door go into the field behind his house, day after day, with a
baseball bat. One by one he tossed stones into the air and hit
them. I might have thought he was just practicing to improve
his ball game if I hadn't caught sight of the pain and anger on
his face. I couldn't hear what he was saying but he was shouting
something with each hit. I later learned that his parents were on
the verge of a divorce. He was frightened, troubled and angry —
the hitting was the only release he dared try.

One mother of five lively, fist-flying youngsters told me of a
technique she developed.

When she saw feelings welling up in one of them she would
say, "Better go down in the cellar and throw some dishes." They
had a choice. They could smash them into a trash barrel kept
nearby for the purpose, or if they wanted to clean up the pieces
afterward, they could throw them against the cellar wall.

"Didn't you ever run out of dishes?" I exclaimed in amazement. "Oh sure," she replied with a grin. "I made a practice of
dropping in at the tail end of a rummage sale and offering to
take off their hands all of the dishes they hadn't sold. They were

usually glad to have that much less to dispose of. I didn't tell them why I wanted them!"

A punching bag or a tackling dummy often serves a dual purpose. It may provide exercise when the weather confines active kids indoors, but it also can be a source of release, as Mark's grandmother discovered.

The director of the nursery school where Mrs. Stokely had placed her two grandchildren stopped her one day when she dropped them off.

"Could you stop for a few minutes after you leave the children?" Miss Sullivan asked. When she returned and they were comfortably seated, she went on to explain. "I was wondering whether there might be something unusual going on in your home. We have noticed quite a change in Mark's behavior recently."

"What is he doing?" Mark's grandmother asked, anxiously.

"Well, he has always been an energetic little fellow, a typical four-year-old, but lately he has been very rough, hurting other children, and when he is corrected he shouts at the teachers or bursts into tears. I thought you might be able to help us understand what is troubling him."

Mrs. Stokely looked for a moment as if *she* might burst into tears. "Yes, we are having some problems," she began, "and I don't know how to handle them. As you know, when Jean, my daughter, was divorced she came home to live with us, bringing Mark and little Jeannie. It has not worked out very well. My husband is a retired army officer who believes in strict discipline. He expects so much of the children," she said with a sigh. "They resent it and so does Jean. I feel as if I am in the middle all the time."

"Was he as strict when your own children were small?" Miss Sullivan asked.

"Yes, but he was not home much of the time. After the children were in school I thought it best for them to be settled in one place so we did not go with him and when he was on leave they managed to stay out of his way. It's different now. He is

home all of the time. He acts more like a drill sergeant than a
loving grandfather! He wants them to be quiet and obedient and
jump the minute he speaks to them. In a way I can see that it is
hard on him—he looked forward to retirement and they do get
on his nerves when they act silly or squabble. Mark gets into
things. The other day he spilled some paint in my husband's
workshop and I thought Jim would have a heart attack. It could
be that Mark is missing his father, but he never asks about him
so we don't talk about it."

"Perhaps you need to give him a chance to talk," Miss
Sullivan suggested. "Sometimes we jump to conclusions about
what is going on in a child's mind and find that we are way off
base."

"There is one thing that has changed," Mrs. Stokely
continued. "Jean has started dating again. I don't believe that
can be the problem because Mark adores Bill. He would
monopolize all of his time when he visits if he could. And Bill is
very good about giving him attention. They play ball and
sometimes he gets down on the floor and wrestles with him. That
irks my husband, too."

"There are a few things I can suggest which might ease the
situation, and give Mark an outlet for whatever is really
bothering him," Miss Sullivan offered. "When we are sure of
that we will know how to help him."

"I'll try anything as long as I can keep him out of Jim's
way," Mrs. Stokely replied.

"For starters, why don't you try a punching bag. Stuff a
pillow case or laundry bag with old rags and hang it up where
the children play."

"We have fixed up a playroom in the basement," Mrs.
Stokely interjected.

"That's good. Now the next time Mark seems upset, you
might suggest that he can work it out on the punching bag."

"Well, I'll try it," was the dubious reply.

Two days later she came into the office. "It worked!" she
exclaimed. "And you were right. I was jumping to the wrong
conclusion. It wasn't Jim's strictness that was upsetting Mark."

"What was it, then?" Miss Sullivan queried, smiling.

"The punching bag you suggested gave me the answer," said
Mrs. Stokely. "I hung it up downstairs in the playroom, and

when Mark went down to use it, I sat on the top step and listened. He was talking all the while he gave that pillow a real going-over and this is what he said."

"You are an old meanie! You come here and take my mother to all those nice places and you don't take me!" He went on and on. Apparently he is not jealous because someone is paying attention to his mother; he is jealous because she is getting the attention he wants from this young man. Now that we know what it is, I think they can handle it, make it clear that he can go with them some of the time, but that they also want time alone.

A punching bag can be used in the nursery school or at home. The children can help to make it, stuffing a pillow case or a large paper shopping bag with dry leaves, nylon stockings, straw — whatever is at hand.

"When my babies are fretful we sit down and have a great time tearing up newspaper," a teacher of toddlers in a child care center related. "Then we stuff them into paper bags. I tie the end and we pretend that they are snow balls and throw them. Another time when we had filled a big bag, I hung it up and we

took turns hitting it with a stick, the way Spanish children do with a piñata at Christmas time."

Tearing cloth is another way to release feelings. There is something about the sound—as well as the motion—which feels good! Joseph's teacher (Chapter III) kept a pile of worn-out men's shirts on a shelf in a closet for this purpose. On more than one occasion Joseph vented his wrath on them! The pieces need not be thrown away! They can be used to stuff punching bags! Long strips can be used to teach braiding.

For older children, a store bought punching bag or tackling dummy may be a good investment.

Pounding

Pounding is another means of release. In one child care center, I saw a tree stump. A small child was standing beside it pounding nails with very large heads into it. "That is our pounding place," his teacher said when she saw me looking at it. "It really makes you feel good to bang those nails with a hammer."

"What do you do when there's no room for more nails?" I asked.

"Someone takes them all out at the end of each day," she replied. "It isn't as if we were destroying something they created—it's the pounding that is important."

For very little children pounding clay serves the same purpose. Before they acquire the skill for sculpture there is a lot of pounding, rolling, manipulating. I knew one teacher who, when she sensed things were getting out of hand, would quietly set up a table with clay boards and some good moist clay, and gently direct the fractious ones to it.

Painting Is More Than Art

Emotions do not always have to be expressed with violent action. For some people art is a medium of expression. Feelings can flow out, rather than erupt. It is well known that Prime Minister Winston Churchill, and President Dwight D. Eisenhower, two men who bore the burden of enormous reponsibility, found time to paint pictures, and one has to assume that it served them as a release from pressure and tension.

Danny, the same little boy who wrote to his grandmother about the poison berries, had another problem to confront later in the same year. His father was going to the hospital for an operation on his eye. His parents were worried—but they thought they had been successful in concealing their anxiety from Danny.

One day his mother called the teacher. "I have a place set up in the laundry room where Danny can play with messy materials, like clay and paint; the stuff I don't want in his room or in my kitchen. Yesterday when I was doing the wash, he was playing with his fingerpaints. He chose black and brown. I could hear him muttering, so I listened and he was saying, 'That's the gucky, mucky hospital where my dad is going!' Apparently he had heard more than we realized. We have talked it all over with him, and I think he feels better now."

A nursery school teacher told this story of helping a child talk out his problems.

Jason's father was asked to come to the school for a conference. Jason had become very withdrawn; he was not taking part in any of the activities which he had previously enjoyed, and he rebuffed any overtures made by the teachers or children. This little boy's mother died when he was two, and after a succession of housekeepers, his father had married again.

When the director described Jason's behavior, his father said, "That certainly is different from the way he is acting at home. Instead of being quiet, he is obnoxious; interrupting when we are talking, running wildly through the house when we have company, and deliberately breaking things. He has nightmares—and has even started wetting the bed, something he stopped doing long ago."

"Could it be that he doesn't like the idea of your remarrying?" the director ventured.

"I don't think so," the father replied. "When I told him about it he seemed very happy."

The next day the teacher sat down at a low table and invited Jason to join her. Between them was a box of smooth, small, one-inch blocks. Experience had taught her that children's tongues were loosened when their hands were occupied. "Let's see what we can build with these," she said, starting to pile them up. After a few moments, Jason tentatively began to move the blocks around, feeling their smoothness, making patterns. The teacher casually brought up the subject of his new mother. "What do you call her?" she asked. Jason gradually began to talk. Without seeming to realize what he was communicating, he disclosed that he hated his new mother. He didn't really hate her—but if he liked her she would go away—the way his own mother did—and all those other women. Jason was hurting—and relating in the only language he could—through his behavior. When his parents understood the problem they were able to reassure him.

Ruth Taylor Stone, one of the pioneers in early childhood education, told the following story.

"It was the beginning of W.W. II. Rosa, a normally happy little girl came into school one morning, hung up her coat and went straight to the painting easel. There she chose brown, black, and purple, layering one over the other. She used the brush aggressively, scrubbing, jabbing and spattering. An observant teacher moved closer to her and heard her muttering, 'I hope to hell they don't take him!' The next day she came in all smiles, and again went straight to the easel where she painted a beautiful, rainbow-like picture with pastel colors, and her movements were almost a dance as she applied the paint to paper. This time she was singing, 'They didn't take him!' Her father had been called in the draft, but he was rejected."

Painting may work well in the nursery school, but all homes are not set up to accommodate the mess, and many mothers are not temperamentally suited to put up with it.

Water Play—the Most Accessible Material

There is another soothing medium which is readily accessible to everyone—and cost free—water! Perhaps it is because it is free that so many teachers do not take advantage of the therapeutic value water play offers. A homesick child, a lonely or shy child, an emotionally upset child—can find release standing at a sink filled with warm water—just messing around with cups, funnels, strainers, tubes or the gravy baster.

Adding a handful of soapflakes will heighten the experience and an eggbeater may be included in the equipment. A few drops of vegetable coloring or tempera paint will add still more variety.

Reading and Telling Stories

Books offer some children an outlet for the expression of their feelings. As with puppets they live vicariously through identifying with an imaginary person. Only in the last ten years or so have we had access to stories which depict children as they really are. Whole generations of children grew up with the notion that "nice people" didn't experience strong feelings—and if they did they must never show them. Parents didn't kiss or touch each other in the presence of their children. Little boys and girls were led to believe that it was wicked to hate your own brother or sister, and spinster aunts were to be kissed and revered—even when you couldn't stand them. Love was to be delivered on demand—not earned.

Today we have authors like Judith Viorst who write about children as they really are. When we read aloud from books like

"I'll Fix Anthony," and "The Terrible, Horrible, No-Good Very Bad Day" we can almost feel the relief draining out of the listener.

Dorene gave Randy relief when she asked him to tell her how he felt. Making up stories can serve the same purpose. One teacher in an elementary school surprised her pupils when she invited them to write about their feelings.

"Your story doesn't have to be about nice things," she said. "It can be about mean, scary, angry things. About what you think when you feel naughty."

She knew better than to expect much at first. These children had to believe that they could trust her; that their stories would not be used against them. Some people were critical of her method. "You are encouraging bad behavior — condoning it!" they said.

"I believe that mean feelings are better put on paper than in hitting people or smashing things," was her answer.

As the children gained confidence they at first went overboard testing her with obscene words and weird tales of violence. Gradually they shifted over to whimsy and humor. Her cue was to express interest and to avoid criticism. Families can use the written word as a means of expression, also.

When I was teaching a class in "Creative Activities for Children" I gave an assignment which threw some of my students into a panic. "Before the end of the semester," I said, "I will expect each of you to write an original poem."

With audible moans and groans they protested.

"I haven't a creative bone in my body!"

"I don't even like to read poetry — let alone write it!"

"I can see where I'm going to flunk this course!"

By the end of the term some of the most ardent objectors had, to their own surprise, submitted some delightful poems. For example, Carol put the following verse on my desk with a triumphant glow. "I can't believe I really wrote that!" she said.

Electric Jewels

At night when I look out at the city
I see a jewelry display set against
Black velvet before me.

In the distance the street lights
Look like diamond earrings.
The airport runway looks like a queen's tiara.
The red lights on the radio tower
    could be a ruby necklace.
"See," I said to myself, "You
    really don't have to be a millionaire to have jewels.
"You don't even have to be Elizabeth Taylor!"

Another student told of using her assignment to help the family get through a disastrous weekend. "We were all miserable with the flu," she said, "including me. In desperation I told them what you said about anyone being able to write poetry — and everyone tried it — the kids — even my husband. At first some of it was pretty silly. Rhyming junk — but as they shared what they had written — it began to change. I'm going to make a scrapbook of that weekend — and put it away. When the children are older I think they will enjoy it."

Music

Music is another form of therapy which can be used to release feelings and avoid problems. Even very young infants will respond when they are moved in time to music. The young mother who dances around the room with her child in her arms, dipping, swaying, bouncing, singing, is adapting to the natural rhythm which is within the child. More than that she is conveying a sense of joy — which makes the infant feel good!

Teachers can extend this pleasure with a few simple rhythm instruments. Sticks to strike together, a drum, tambourine and triangle, or a pair of cymbals can be associated with feelings. Which one would you choose to say you are angry? Which one would tell me you are happy?

Children at home often turn away from their expensive toys to play with pots and pans found in the kitchen. Two pot lids will substitute for cymbals, an aluminum or stainless steel cover will make a beautiful gong and an assortment of plastic bowls, dishpans and wastebaskets will become resounding drums.

Children have a natural sense of rhythm which will develop as they experiment with instruments accompanied by records.

"It sounds like a lot of work," one mother sighed.

"Some day keep a record of the number of minutes you spend nagging and think about all the energy you use in scolding, and feeling guilty," I replied. "These things I have suggested add up to fun! If you can participate in that fun you will enjoy a new relationship with your children. It's worth a try!"

Dramatic Play Discloses Feelings

The playhouse in child care centers provides a theater for acting out the problems which may be affecting a child's behavior. Teachers need to be as discreet as a priest who hears confessions, because family arguments and other intimate details are often portrayed with painful accuracy. If a child whacks, pinches, and slams around a doll, it is a pretty good clue as to how he really feels about the new baby at home. In this child-sized duplication of the adult world, frightening scenes, reenacted, can lose their terror.

Herman's father was about to be forced out of the store which he and his father before him had occupied because the building had been sold. The dramatic play which Herman instigated day after day demonstrated a little boy's reaction to the anger, frustration and worry his family were experiencing.

Young children will not tell on their parents who may be physically or sexually abusing them, but a discerning teacher can gain some clues to what may be going on if she observes dramatic play. A social worker spoke to the director of a child-care center. "We are taking Gina and Josephine's father to court for child abuse," she said. "Have your teachers heard or seen anything that might be used against him?"

At first, when they were asked, the teachers said that they had nothing to report except that these two little girls were abnormally quiet and withdrawn, and played only with each other. Later Lou went alone to the director. "There is something I have noticed," she said hesitantly. "Until you mentioned this, I hadn't really recognized the significance of it. Every day those two little girls gather up all of the dolls and line them up on the doll's bed—on their stomachs with their bottoms sticking up and their legs hanging over the edge."

A sensitive observer can get an idea of what the world looks like to a child. In most cases the teacher is not expected to interpret her observations; she should relate them to the professional who will know how to convert the child's fantasies into reality.

Another story came from the director of a day camp.

Raymond, aged seven, had his counselors, and fellow campers in a constant state of upheaval. He swore, lied, started fights deliberately and broke every rule. The director was thinking about asking his parents to withdraw him when his counselor discovered the all important key. On a rainy day he told his campers the story of the "Sorcerer's Apprentice" and played the record.

"Do you think we could make that into a show and do it for the rest of the camp?" he asked.

Raymond spoke up quickly, "I'll be the Sorcerer," he

announced. That was a turning point for this child. He threw so much vigor into his part that the rest of the children were spellbound. He became a coach, director, scenery designer, and producer of this and other plays! As he found satisfaction through this and won the admiration of his pals, his whole attitude changed. He was too busy to be naughty! His "I AM" was going full speed ahead!

Most homes have the equipment which can be assembled to create a stage for dramatic play. A small table and chairs, tea sets and discarded cookware, telephones and dress up clothes; when a child is having a behavior problem, an ear tuned in to this corner may offer some clues.

On looking back over this chapter, I see that what I am really saying is that punishment is what we use when our adult emotions get out of hand. The suggestions offered here are ways of dealing with them before punishment is necessary.

Adages last because they condense meaning into a few easily remembered words, and certainly the time-honored saying, "An ounce of prevention is worth a pound of cure," sums up this chapter.

CHAPTER 14

A Piece of
the Action

In the business world there is a commonly used phrase; "a piece of the action." Simply stated it means that an employee who shares in the profits is motivated to work harder. This principle can be applied to the concept of discipline that "*makes sense.*" A family is a corporation. Adults hold the administrative positions, but the business is more likely to succeed when every worker feels like a partner rather than a subordinate. When the children in a family are allowed to participate in making the rules which govern the household, they find it easier to accept them.

Bruce and Sandra Wallace found it necessary to reorganize the corporate structure of their family organization. Since Sandra had gone back to work they were spending too many of the precious hours they had left for their children in arguments and nagging.

The Wallace Corporation—A Family Meeting

The notice on the bulletin board was impressive:
Meeting of the Wallace Corporation
July 25 at 7:30 P.M. Dining Room
"What's it all about?" Ralph asked when he came home from his school.

"I don't know any more than you do," Lola mumbled through her peanut butter and jelly sandwich.

As each of the five Wallace children read the notice, interest and curiosity mounted. When their mother came in from her job at four they plied her with questions which she answered with "You'll see!"

At 7:30, with dinner over and the dishes cleared away, father sat at the head of the table, facing five attentive, expectant children.

"Your mother and I have decided that it is time to let you all get involved in the business of managing a home and family," he announced in serious tones. "We are going to have a family meeting every week. With both of us working, we need to set up some ground rules about taking care of the house, and getting along with each other. Up until now we have made all those rules — and they don't seem to be working very well, so now we want you to help decide what is necessary. Everyone will get a chance to talk — to make suggestions, even little Jimmy, and we will all listen — politely! No put downs, like 'stupid!' or 'that's a dumb idea!'"

"What rules do you think we need?" he asked, and was immediately barraged with heated attacks on past restrictions, everyone trying to talk at the same time.

"We should have bigger allowances!" Ralph got his pet peeve in first.

"I think we should be allowed to go to bed when we are ready!" Lola interjected quickly. "You always make me go when Wilma does, and I am three years older!"

At first, after announcing that everyone would have a voice in making decisions, father's authoritative background got in the way. Discussion was fine, but when push came to shove, it was clear that he intended to have the final word.

When his wife and children complained, he shifted too far in the opposite direction.

"O.K., O.K., try it your way," he grumbled, abdicating his role as leader.

The meeting degenerated into the usual arguments, and ended with father issuing an angry, "Well, I guess you just aren't mature enough yet to take on this kind of responsibility."

There is a certain amount of risk involved in testing democratic procedures. Just as the cart driver who relinquishes the reins entirely may have a runaway horse, the parent who totally abdicates his position of authority may be the reason we have so many runaway children wandering the streets of our cities.

On the other hand, if a driver holds the reins loosely, and gives the horse its head, it is probable that if he fell off the seat, the horse would find its way home. In the same way, if children can be trusted with increasing responsibilities based on mutual understanding, they will be more likely to find their way out of difficult situations.

After Bruce Wallace had taken time to cool down he recognized that part of the learning process is living with the consequences of wrong decisions. There must be flexibility. When rules are made there should be a plan for review and change. Sometimes the adult has to grit his teeth and let children find out—and sometimes he needs to demonstrate the meaning of mediation and compromise.

Family meetings can serve several purposes. They can make life easier because they provide a forum for communication and reduce the need for nagging and arguments. They also can teach the child the principles of democracy. However, before attempting to institute the process, parents should come to an agreement with each other about what they are trying to accomplish and how they will proceed.

It would be naive to suggest that the Wallace family meetings solved all of their problems overnight. It took several meetings, patient persistence and a determination to make it work before all of the members of the family acknowledged that it really was a good idea.

The issues they resolved come up in every family.

A suggestion on the matter of bedtime was to try letting each child decide when he would go to bed, but to insist that he must get up at the usual time the next day, and fulfill all of his expected responsibilities. Relieved of the need to rebel against parental edicts, many children will choose to go to bed earlier.

The decision on allowances depends somewhat on the parents' willingness to share the facts. If children can understand that there is just so much money to spend, and that if it is given in allowances there may not be enough for some of the taken-for-granted luxuries—they can accept the restrictions.

However, parents need to be fair. If there really is enough, and if
the family is functioning as a corporation, bigger allowances
may be justified.

Allowances

Connie, a single parent who was struggling to bring up
three children alone after their father died was driven to include
her children in sharing her financial problems.

"Mom, I have to have thirty dollars tomorrow for a new pair
of track shoes," Harry announced as he came in the back door.

"How much did you say?" Connie Martin responded from
the kitchen.

"Thirty dollars," was the answer.

"Thirty dollars!" Connie shrieked. "You have to be crazy! Do
you kids think I'm made of money? Have you any idea how hard
I work just to put food on the table, and to buy you clothes?"

"But I have to have them!" Harry persisted. "Coach says I
can't run until I get them, and the competition is coming up next
month!"

"Then let the coach buy them!" Connie answered irritably.
"I haven't had a new pair of shoes for a whole year—and I am
NOT going to pay out thirty dollars so you can run! You'll just
have to get into some other sport that isn't so expensive. Ask for
a longer paper route—and get your exercise doing something
useful!"

It was the end of a hard day at the office and Connie Martin
was feeling sorry for herself.

"The rest of the girls in the office went out to dinner
together tonight and they are going to see that great show
afterward. They asked me to go but I can't afford it! Instead,
here I am standing over a hot stove trying to make a cheap
nourishing meal look appetizing. Sure, I lost my temper, and I
hate myself for it, but that kid always picks the worst possible
time to come at me asking for money!"

She served up the meal in tight-lipped silence, and the
children, taking their cue from her expression, ate without
talking. With an eye to making amends, Connie piled generous

servings of ice cream on the pie she had made on the previous Sunday and then managed an apologetic smile.

"I'm sorry I yelled at you, Harry," she began. "I was tired and because I couldn't go out with the rest of the girls in the office, I took it out on you. I guess we can manage to find the money for the shoes.

"I wish we could find a better system," she went on. "Sometimes when you kids ask me for money I give it to you because I am too busy or too tired to argue, so I just give it to you and then I feel guilty and resentful. Then other times I yell at you, the way I did tonight and say 'NO' when you really need it and that makes me feel terrible.

"Now after supper I want you, Harry and Susan, to make a list of everything you can think of that you have to have money for, like bus fares and lunch money, and I am going to give you an allowance to take care of them. Then I will look at my budget and see how much I can give you for the things you couldn't plan for in advance. You will have to live within that allowance, and earn whatever you need for extras.

"I have to budget the money that I earn to pay the rent, the lights, gas and phone bills, food and car payments. I have to leave some for the things which keep coming up like new clothes or a visit to the dentist, or something like Harry's track shoes. I think you are old enough, and smart enough to learn how to manage your own budgets and if it keeps me from turning into a nagging old witch, it will be worth trying."

"Aw, you're not so bad!" Harry conceded. "But I do like the idea of an allowance. I hate having to come asking you for every little thing!"

Should an allowance be considered payment for daily chores about the home? In my opinion they are separate issues. Every member of the household who enjoys its benefits should carry some responsibility for maintaining it. They should see it as "our home" rather than a free hotel; the more they invest in that home the greater their pride will be. Making their own beds, emptying the trash, helping with the laundry and dishes should not be matters for discussion and argument. When parents offer an allowance for these simple daily tasks they are really offering a choice on something that should be taken for granted.

As the children grow older and their financial needs increase, an allowance can be presented as "your fair share of the family income." This will teach the child money management and relieve the tensions caused by nagging and arguments.

Four year olds are capable of participating in making rules for behavior as Mrs. Clancy, a teacher in the child care center, discovered.

Democracy in the Classroom

It was near the end of a long cold winter and the children had been cooped up indoors more than they could tolerate. The tempo and noise level of the classroom had been steadily climbing, and Mrs. Clancy heard her own voice adding to the tumult. After a particularly hard day she went home with a severe headache, and out of desperation conceived a plan. (Note: Good teachers do not work nine to five. They do their most constructive planning when they are away from the distractions of the children.)

Arriving at school the next morning she arranged the chairs in rows — theater style.

When Pauline's father dropped her off the child stood looking at the chairs in surprise.

"What is that for?" she asked. "What are we going to do? Are we having a show?

"No," Mrs. Clancy replied. "We are having a meeting."

That was a familiar word. Parents attended meetings and sometimes teachers had to leave the classroom to go to a meeting.

Pauline took it upon herself to explain to each arrival, 'We are going to have a meeting!"

Some of them sat down immediately — assuming a serious posture. When everyone was ready Mrs. Clancy called the others over, and sat down in front of them.

"Things have not been very good around here lately!" she began. "I went home yesterday with a terrible headache. Does anyone know why?"

Her audience responded with giggles, solemn nods and sly grins.

"Do you know what laws are?" was her next question.

"Yeah, like don't drive too fast or you get a ticket," Mike spoke up.

"And you can't steal!" Harry interjected.

"And you shouldn't shoot people!" Mary said with a solemn expression.

"What kind of laws could we make for our schoolroom?" Mrs. Clancy asked.

The answers came back thick and fast.

"Don't run indoors!"

"Don't yell!"

"Don't bump into people!"

"Don't take a toy away from someone while they are still playing with it!"

"Put the toys away after you finish playing with them!"

"Those are all good laws," Mrs. Clancy said approvingly. "Let's write them down." She printed them on a large sheet of paper and numbered them, at the same time reading each one aloud.

"Which one says don't run?" she asked.

"Number 5," Donny said, stepping up to point to it.

"Who knows what number seven says?" was her next question.

After they played that game for awhile, she asked, "Can anyone think of another way to use these laws?"

"Well, if one kid sees another running, he could say 'Number 5'!" Sylvia said.

"Or you could just hold up four fingers and we would know it is 'Don't yell'!" Billy chimed in.

"Hey, how would it be if we put the numbers in a box, and when someone breaks a law you could tell them to go find the right number?" Orlo suggested.

By the time they were through offering their ideas, most of the children had the rules very well in mind. They had learned them because they had a need and a desire to know, a basic requirement for learning and retention. This whole experiment in democracy became a good reading-readiness lesson, far more valuable than sitting at a table, filling in spaces in workbooks!

The teacher who starts this democratic process early in the school year will be able to devote her time and energy to "real teaching" as the year progresses. Children are quite capable of assuming far more responsibility for their own actions than we give them credit for.

On the other hand, weary, frazzled teachers who still find themselves nagging, repeating orders and scolding over trivia in January may be able to use the "meeting" to pull themselves out of the hole. It is a way of making their expectations known and finding a system for restoring order to chaos.

As we pursue our goal of *"helping children to see the sense in acting a certain way,"* we must give them the freedom — and the tools — to express their thoughts, fears and anxieties as well as their moments of joy and delight.

Honest Listening

The first step in teaching the art of communication is to listen! Really listen! Even a very young child knows when you only pretend to pay attention to what he is saying. If you nod your head, answering with an occasional word or grunt, while your mind is occupied on another channel, his radar system will tell him. When you put him off with:

"Don't bother me now. Can't you see I am busy?"

"Go tell your father."

"That's nice."

He will quickly get the message that you have left your receiver "off the hook."

Honest listening means that you are willing to let your child say some things you would rather not hear. If your son tells you in confidence that his chum is stealing money from his mother's purse, you have a problem you would rather not deal with. Are you going to tell your neighbor and risk making an enemy? On the other hand, if you can earn the trust of your child at an early age, so that he feels safe sharing his confidences, you will reap the benefits when the difficult years of adolescence come.

It isn't enough, however, for your child to have faith in you. Somehow you must convey the idea that you have faith in him! Years ago I attended a lecture by Mary Fisher Langmuir, who was then on the faculty of Vassar College.

"How can you expect your children to have faith in themselves," she asked, "unless they *know* you have faith in them?" I do not remember anything else that she said—I am not even sure what her subject was—but that one sentence made a permanent impression on my mind. More than once as my children were growing, I was grateful for that bit of advice!

"Talk—It—Over" Chairs

In one of the many child care centers I have visited, I met a teacher who had developed a method for helping children solve their own "people" problems. It began one day when two little boys were fighting over a truck. Pulling two small chairs together she sat them down, facing each other, and with knees touching. "These are the 'Talk It Over Chairs'," she said. "We are going to learn how to use words instead of fighting when we have a problem.

"Robert, you punched Tom because he tried to take the truck.

"Tom, tell Robert why you wanted the truck.

"No, Robert, it's Tom's turn to talk first. You will have a chance when he is through."

"He wasn't playing with it. He put it down, and I was waiting for it," Tom said.

"But I wasn't through with it," Robert sputtered. "I just left it a minute to go get the gas pump."

The conversation went back and forth, with the teacher standing by, interrupting only when she had to remind them to talk one at a time. They finally arrived at a compromise — and walked away to continue their play happily.

After the "talk-it-over-chairs" had been used successfully several times, this teacher tried a second stage.

"Donna, you and Beverly seem to be having some difficulty," she said. "Why don't you try the 'talk-it-over-chairs'?"

Solemnly, and with great dignity, Donna and Beverly carried out their own negotiations.

The real reward came on another day when two children, without any suggestion from this teacher, arranged the chairs, sat down, and carried through the 'talk-it-over' process to a satisfactory conclusion!

Could some of these methods be applied in the home? With so many families in which two parents are working, communication becomes more of a problem. With family members coming and going, each on a different schedule, it would be hard to find a time for a regularly scheduled meeting, but the pay-off is worth the effort, as the Wallace family discovered.

Tape Recorders

In a world where communication is a science as well as an art, there are other ways to convey messages which may have great appeal for the child who is tuned in to gadgets. With a bit of imagination the tape recorder can serve this purpose.

I knew one mother who left messages on the tape which her son listened to when he came home after school, and who also encouraged him to use the recorder as a sounding board for his feelings about his day, since she couldn't be waiting with the cookies and milk and a listening ear. "A poor substitute," some will say, but it seemed to work very well in that situation. Sometimes he wiped it out after he had let off steam; sometimes he asked her to listen and on other occasions they listened together.

In another family, the bulletin board was the common resource for communication. Each child looked for messages when he came home, and tacked up messages or notes of interest like "I got an A on my test!" or "I've gone to Jack's house to get some help with my math."

Mother took care that her messages were not all directives:

"Thank you for changing the sheets on your bed!"

"Uncle Harry called and invited us to go out on his boat Sunday!"

"Get your homework done early. I have a surprise planned for tonight!"

At first glance it may seem to some readers that the idea of including children in the business of family decisions is too "far out." What it really adds up to is treating children like intelligent human beings. We need to remind ourselves that we do not own them, they are loaned to us. If someone gives you temporary custody of a cherished treasure, you expect to hand it over in at least as good condition as that in which you received it.

When we are dealing with the lives of young children, our obligation extends far beyond that.

CHAPTER 15

Wrong Way! Turn Back!

Not long ago as I was driving on a major highway, I allowed myself to get too preoccupied with thoughts for this book and suddenly found myself facing the sign: WRONG WAY! TURN BACK! Traffic was not heavy at the time and I was able to extricate myself from the problem without too much difficulty. How nice it would have been, I thought, if I could have encountered some similar warning signs when I was bringing up my children!

If you have read this far, you have probably recognized yourself on some of the preceding pages. Did you like what you saw? When I made my mistake on the highway, I had no options, I had to back down and take a different road. As a parent or teacher you have a choice. You can stiffen your back and state unequivocally, "I don't *need* this! All this talk about feelings and letting off steam is just more of that permissive stuff! I just want my kids to be decent, law abiding, God fearing citizens, who respect their elders, and that means they have to learn to do what they are told!"

On the other hand, you might say in a more reflective manner, "I really love my kids, but no one would ever believe that if they heard me yelling at them. I try to do what is best for them but when I discipline them, I feel like a tyrant. The books all say I should be enjoying them, but just when I try to be nice and have a little fun, they do some crazy thing that makes me mad and we are enemies again. I'd like to change directions, but how do I begin?"

A Plan for Change

You have taken the first step when you recognize that behavior problems are never black or white, right or wrong, but, as I said in the beginning, stem from a mixture of people, environment and circumstances. The part of parenting called "Discipline" is a learned skill, and there are plenty of so-called experts eager to help you. Your newspapers, magazines, radio and T.V. offer a smorgasbord of advice. Out of the rich, and sometimes indigestible fare you can select that which seems palatable. That which you retain and digest will become your own personal philosophy for child rearing. You will know it is right because it will "set well." You can never follow exactly in the footsteps of a Dr. Spock, or Dr. Hyam Ginott — or even a Dr. Grace Mitchell; but rather you take something from each one and build your own composite. The key is to have an open mind, listen, observe, sift the evidence and draw your own conclusions. We are living at a time when games are big — not just for children but for the whole family. That same problem-solving energy can be applied to the fascinating challenge of discipline. Unlike the Rubik's cube there is no absolute final solution when you are dealing with people relationships, but there is always *another chance.*

Look at Your Own "I AM"

In an interview once I was asked, "Would you do anything different if you were bringing up children today?" That was an intriguing thought. My response had to begin with "How am *I* different?" It was very plain that the greatest change in my attitudes, and in my own self development came when I absorbed the "I AM!" "I CAN!" concept.

With that as my guide, I know that if I were "parenting" now I would be able to look at the causes of behavior rather than the deeds; that I would read the messages my children were conveying in their own language. My goals would be different because I would be more concerned about helping them to develop a strong "I AM" than in having them become models of good behavior who would reflect credit on me!

If you asked me where to begin on a plan for changing your direction, I would have to say, "With your own self concept." Putting modesty aside, and knowing that your list will never be scrutinized or graded, make up a balance sheet of your strengths and your weaknesses. For example:

I yell a lot   *but*   We do have some good laughs together.

I make my kids   *but*   They always know
toe the mark   where they stand.

This gives you something concrete to work on. Once you have acknowledged your weaknesses, you can tackle them, one at a time. Don't expect to change overnight. Nibble away at them—and someday you will realize that you have taken a big bite!

How Were You Disciplined?

The next step to think about is the way you were treated when you were growing up. Were your parents too harsh? Too lenient? How were you disciplined? Did it accomplish the best results? Were you left filled with resentment, promising yourself never to treat your children that way? How well do you adhere to that resolve now? We have a tendency to perpetuate the mistakes of those who went before us. Are you spanking, yelling, shaming, piling guilt on your kids because that is the way it was done to you? Or have you gone to the other extreme, of being overly indulgent—subconsciously trying to even the score?

If you are a teacher think back through the years of your schooling. How many of your teachers left a clear impression on you? How many can you name? Recall a visual image? Are you surprised to find how few come clearly to mind? If your memories are strong, was it because they were a good influence or so mean that you still get a tight feeling inside when you think about them? Are your fondest recollections those of teachers who ran a tight ship? Who made their expectations clear and enforced the rules?

My husband, a high school teacher for many years, had a

reputation for being very strict. I'm sure the students referred to him as "Old Man Mitchell" and worse, just as I remember teachers who were always dubbed "Biddy...." Nevertheless, people come up to him now on the street and at social gatherings and say, "You won't remember me, but I had you for a teacher at Newton High. I thought you were pretty mean and tough — but I learned more from you than any other teacher I ever had. I didn't dare try any funny business — but you were always fair!"

It saddens me when I see teachers in child care who seem to have their notions of discipline encased in cement. "Get in line!" "Sit still!" "Apologize!" "Be quiet!!!" "When will you grow up?" and I can easily visualize the teachers that taught them!

I am reminded of a phrase I once heard, "Teachers of young children take the wriggling, squirming little humans in their care and manipulate all the joy out of their lives!"

When you have passed through the first stage — reaffirming your own "I AM", you will be able to acknowledge that you are making the mistake of carrying on with someone else's methods — and shift into your own teaching style.

What Kind of Adults Do You Want Your Children to Be?

Now that you have looked at the present, and the past, get out your crystal ball and look into the future. What kind of adults do you want your children or pupils to be? You have a vested interest in that answer — because they are going to be the decision makers who will some day decide what is going to happen to you. Old age is in some ways a replay of infancy. Most of us do end our days in a dependent state. Even though you may be wise enough to cover yourself financially, you can't guarantee that your money will buy you good care! What if the mistakes you are making now are being recorded — to be returned as my son did, "spank for spank?" A horrible thought, but not as far out as it may seem.

We have known about child abuse for a long time, but only in recent years have we begun to hear about "parent abuse." It exists, and is seldom exposed for the same reasons. Dependent old folks as well as dependent children are afraid to speak up against their only source of "security." And it isn't just the aged who are abused. With the increasing number of single parent families I have known of many women who are afraid to discipline their children, even husky kindergarteners who are strong enough to fight back and really hurt!

What kind of people will be the best guardians of our future? Will the way we treat our children produce the results we want?

Next I suggest that you refer once more to the definition, which I believe is the cornerstone of positive disciplinary practices. It points the way to self discipline, and a person who is in control of himself is a self confident, competent individual who knows who he is, where he wants to go, and how to get there. It also stresses that *helping a child* is a *slow, bit-by-bit, time-consuming task*. It is an investment — and the rewards will come when you receive the interest. When my children were old enough to do extraordinary things for me and I would express my gratitude, they answered, "Just the interest on your investment!"

And if you do decide to make that kind of an investment, how will you know when you are making progress? When the day comes that you can step into the skin of the child who is antagonizing you; when you can concentrate on the "why" of his behavior, rather than the deed itself it is as if some magical process takes over. You reach a new level of maturity and self confidence. Like all real magic it is difficult to explain — but when it happens to you, you will know it!

It's Later Than You Think!

It can't stop there! Don't ever think you have it made! You will need to keep up your strength and continued growth with what I call educational vitamins. Attend a lecture or a workshop, read a new book or reread an old one with a new perspective. Keep your viewpoint fresh and feisty — and enjoy your children! It's later than you think!

CHAPTER 16

In a Nutshell

I have presented many ideas in this book—any one of which could be a subject for discussion. To summarize, let me extract from them a few "pearls of wisdom" which are so basic that the reader might shrug and say, "Of course! Anyone knows that!" but they bear repeating.

If each of these rules was practiced, parents and teachers would find their lives easier, and children could enjoy the years of childhood to which they are entitled.

1. Start a planned program for discipline at a very early age. The years before six are the best years for learning. Problems which develop then can be resolved as easily as pulling out a long basting thread. Trying to help a child of seven or eight who is already messed up is more like picking at the tiny threads of machine stitching.

2. Find something to love in every child. I know it is hard if he is dirty, smelly, swears at you or hits you, but it is your job to keep trying!

3. Make certain that every child finds some small measure of success every day and praise him for it. It may be, "I see that you are trying to remember to close the door quietly", but he needs encouragement if his "I AM" is going to feed his "I CAN" and keep that wheel spinning in a positive direction.

4. Be fair and consistent. Weaving back and forth pulls the rug out from under a child's feet. If it is right today and not tomorrow; if he is smothered with love at one moment and severely punished the next without understanding what he may have done to deserve it, life becomes very confusing. The scars left on his developing personality may never heal.

5. Avoid labeling. "The child becomes what he sees in your eyes!" If you constantly tell him that he is "stupid", a "slowpoke", "sneaky", "a liar", or a "mean kid", you will start him on the way to fitting that label.

6. Parents and teachers cooperate! You have a common goal! Teachers can share what they have learned from working with large numbers of children, but only the parents know about all of the factors which come together to make their child a unique personality.

Have faith in each other! Trust and respect each other, and the child will be the winner!

Index

Adjustment
  to work environment, 119
  to new baby, 72–73
  when new baby becomes "cute", 74
Admitting mistakes
  child, 85, 86
  parent, 106
  teacher, 84
Allowances, 137–140
Anticipate
  as a teacher, 8
  before arrival of new baby, 77–78
  explanation of, 8
  parents, to avoid problems, 13
  when mother is child's teacher,
    110
Apologies
  parent to child, 91, 92
  teacher to child, 92–95
  teacher to class, 84
Approval
  child's need for, 36, 118
Arguing
  children with parents, 45, 97, 117,
    136

Bedtime
  a reasonable solution, 137
  rules for, 44
Behavior
  as second language, 26, 27, 31
  biting, 52
  clues to, 19
  regressive, 110, 128
  understanding of, 19, 30
Biting, 49–54
  age differences, 52
  because of sibling jealousy, 73
  never bite back, 54
  seeking clues through observation,
    23, 51
  supervision to prevent, 53, 74

Books and stories
  as outlet for expression of feelings,
    29–31
  before arrival of new baby, 77–78
  in teaching value of truth, 58
Bribes
  are like blackmail, 90
  for eating, 39
Bulletin board
  to improve communication, 145
Buying time, 15, 16, 83

Child abuse
  clues seen in dramatic play, 132
  not always physical, 35
  spanking without self-control, 113
Change, 148–151
Choices
  implied in threats, 83
  living with wrong choice, 86
  offering opportunities for, 85
  parents have, 147
  when there are no choices, 84
Clay
  as means of releasing hostility, 127
Communication
  as a skill, 26
  bulletin board, 145
  caregivers to infants, 26
  child's confusion over meanings, 25
  child's second language, 26
  first step is to listen, 142
  home to school, 30–31
  in family meetings, 137
  parent to child, 30
  positive directions, 27
  problem for working parents, 144
  spoken word best tool, 25
  tape recorder, 144
  teacher to parent, 12
  with child about biting, 53
  with parents about biting, 51–52

Comparisons, 88–89
Competition, 88–89
    compete against self, 90
    emotional strain, 90
    in a competitive society, 90
    related to age, 90
Confrontation
    child with teacher, 15, 27
    over eating, 39
    over natural routines, 37
Consistency
    adults find hard to maintain, 36
    basic rule for success, 153
    dealing with temper, 68–69
    how to achieve, 36
    in rules for bedtime, 43–44
    key to behavior management, 13
    lack of destroys trust, 33
Courtesy
    parent for child, 36, 40

Decision making
    important training, 85
Definition (of discipline)
    and apologizing, 95
    cornerstone of discipline, 15
    biting, 54
    feelings, 117
    lying, 58
    obscenity, 61
    meetings, 135, 142
    on prevention of problems, 117
    on punishment, 105
Democracy
    in classrooms, 140–142
    in family, 135–137
Development
    ages and stages, 102
    reasonable expectations, 20
    teachers can help parents, 76
Diary, 102
Dictating
    child's letter, 75
    to relieve feelings, 120–121
Discipline
    and parenting, 148
    "because I say so", 45

child can accept when fair, 150
    common ideas of, 2
    definition of, 2
    for obscenity, 64
    parent as tyrant, 147
    parents create own problems, 81
    problems caused by jealousy, 79
    self-discipline, 1, 4
    stems from own experience, 149
Diversionary tactics
    for screaming, 67
    for throwing things, 65
Dramatic play
    as means of improving behavior,
        134
    discloses children's feelings, 132
    housekeeping center, 21
    in the home environment, 134
Dressing
    letting child do it, 45

Eating
    in group, 8, 37–38, 41
    in home, 38–41
    natural process, 37
Eliminating (toileting)
    natural process, 37
    when it becomes a problem, 43
Environment
    cause of behavior, 20–21
    in center, 12
    for eating, 39–42
    in home, 23, 46
Expectations
    based on own experience, 148–149
    grandparents of child, 123
    of teachers in your past, 149–150
    parents, 148

Feelings
    and attitudes toward obscenity, 61
    anger, ways to control, 15–16
    caused by biting, 53
    child left to handle alone, 114
    fear, child's reaction to, 30
    helping child to recognize, 117
    jealousy of new baby, 71–77, 79

legitimate means of releasing, 66,
123, 126, 129, 144
not "nice" to have, 129
of working parents, 101
parents have right to, 34
putting self into child's skin, 5, 17,
30, 151
repressing, 69, 76, 117
school age write about, 120, 130
the "put down", 86–88
Frank, Dr. Lawrence, 3
Frustration
in child, caused by teacher, 119
of parent, 12, 106
of single, working parent, 138
reason for biting, 51
when teacher has own child in
class, 111

Ginott, Dr. Hyam, 148
Guilt
child, for biting, 75
child, for obscenity, 32
of working parents, 102, 139
parents, 34
piling on child, 149

Hall, Dr. Volta
new baby, 71–72
What will "they" think?, 5
Hesitate, 16, 30

I AM, I CAN
a philosophy that works, xvii
a basic rule for success, 153
first step toward change, 148, 150
for positive reinforcement, 118
putting it into reverse, 89
Investigate
before blaming, 29–30
for parents, 23
people problems, 19
when child bites, 23, 51
when toileting is a problem, 43
Isolation
when a child bites, 53

Jealousy
child of mother's boyfriend, 125
covering up, 75
delayed feelings of, 73–74
of child when mother is a teacher,
109–110
of new baby, 71–77
parents' solution, 74
Jumping to conclusions
about child's behavior, 124
pertaining to lying, 55

Langmuir, Mary Fisher, 142
Language
age differences, 63–64
and lying, 55
bathroom talk, 62
behavior is second, 26, 27, 31
cultural practices, 60–61
gives sense of power, 27
giving the child words to use, 62
unacceptable, 60
Lear, Edward
Nonsense Alphabet, 62, 63
Learning
basic rule, 61, 141
continual process, 8–9
early years crucial, 153
to live with wrong decisions, 86, 137
Linkletter, Art, 86
Listening
honest listening, 142
to children, 108
to tape recorder, 144
Love
key to trust, 35
self-love, introduction
something in every child, 153
Lying
adults set pattern, 57
causes, 59
to avoid punishment, 58
versus imagination, 54
When is it a lie?, 57

Manners
at meals, 41

grow out of feelings, 91
Meetings
    family, 135–138
    in classroom, 140–142
Montessori method
    sense of order, 47
Music, 131–132

Nagging, 96, 97, 132, 135, 139, 142
Name calling, 3, 154
New baby
    jealousy of, 71–77
    preparing child in advance, 77–78

Observation
    keeping a diary, 102
    of child behavior, 51
Order
    as it leads to learning, 47
"Or elses", 105

Painting
    as means of expression, 126, 128
Parent Abuse, 68, 150–151
Parent-teacher relationships
    about biting, 51
    helping parent anticipate
        problems, 12, 13
    need to understand each other, 103
    teacher with working parents, 101
Permissiveness, 147
    causes child anxiety, 38
Planning
    by teacher, 8, 140
    children share in, 72–73
    in anticipation of new baby, 77–78
    program for discipline, 153
Poetry
    adults use to express feelings, 131
    child uses to express feelings, 120
Positive direction
    director to staff, 101–102
    teacher to child, 27
Positive reinforcement, 68, 102, 117
Pounding
    as means of releasing hostility,
        126–127

Praise
    as a reward, 13
    as positive reinforcement, 11, 89
    earned, 90–91
    for helping with new baby, 78
    for table manners, 41
    when child exerts self-control, 68
Pressure cooker, 119
Problem solving
    child to child, 143
    discipline as a challenge, 148
    parent needs imagination, 108
Program, 22–23
Punching bag
    as means of releasing hostility, 124
Punishment
    children can accept if fair, 115
    for lying, 58
    form of aggression, 36
    if inconsistent, unfair, 53
    relieves adult frustration, 134
    to fit the crime, 89, 115
Puppets
    as means of expression, 121

Quiet places
    where child can be alone, 21, 114

Reading readiness
    an example of, 141
Reading stories
    in preparing for new baby, 77
    in relation to lying, 58
    to help verbal communication, 129
Referrals
    about toileting, 43
    to pediatrician about biting, 51
Regression
    wetting bed, 110, 128
    when new baby comes, 79
Rejection
    of child, when mother is her
        teacher, 111
Resources
    inner, 10
    people to call on, 103

Respect
  key to trust, 35
  parents and teachers for each other,
    154
  parent for child's intelligence, 145
Responsibility
  children in classrooms, 142
  children in home, 137, 139, 140
  for helping with baby, 78
  never-ending for parents, 12
  parents for children, 145
Rewards
  after earned, 90
  for eating, 39
  gold stars, 91
  praise for helping, 13
Riley, Sue Spayth, 83
Role model
  adult displaying temper, 68
  adults set tone of behavior, 118
  in use of unacceptable language,
    64
  lying before child, 57
  parent teaches honesty, 60
  teacher, 15–16
Rules
  as compared to laws, 141
  basic rules for learning, 61
  children help make, 141
  for bedtime, 44
  for eating, 41–42
  for games involving throwing, 65
  for parents and teachers, 153–154
  plan for review and change, 137
  set ground rules, 36

Safety
  in play, 65
Saucy talk
  adults sometimes encourage, 36
Scolding
  parents after bad report from
    teacher, 101
  when parent has own child in class,
    109
Screaming
  diversionary tactics, 67

Security
  from parents, 5
  through consistency, 13
Self-concept, 149
Self-confidence, Intro.
Self-control
  in teacher, 15
  lack of in adult, 3, 113
  lack in child, 94, 114
  suggestions to help child, 15–16
  teaching child importance of, 94
Self-discipline, 151
Sense of humor
  in time of crisis, 84
Separation
  as punishment, 115
  child in center, 115
Setting limits
  children need, 97
  for choices, 85
  for punishment, 116
  offers security, 106
Skills for daily living
  as important as curriculum, 46
Sleeping
  child who goes into parents' bed, 44
  naptime in center, 8, 38
  natural process, 37
  rules for bedtime at home, 44
  wandering through house at night,
    44–45
Spanking, 106–109, 113
Spock, Dr. Benjamin, 148
Stealing
  age related, 59
  parent teaches honesty by example,
    60
Stone, Ruth Taylor, 128
Supervision
  teacher to aide, 95
  when a child bites, 53, 74
Support
  call in reserves, 103
  day care supports parents, 101
  director to parent, 103
  director to teacher, 103–104
  parent for child, 68

supervisor to director, 51, 99–103
teacher to teacher, 10

Talk-it-over chairs, 103
Tape recorders
    to improve communication, 144
Tearing
    as means of releasing hostility, 126
Temper Tantrums
    different kinds, 67–68
    Joseph, 15–16
Testing
    child-parent, 111
    democratic procedures, 136
"They"
    child's concept of adults, 93
    for parents, 5
    for teachers, 37
    when teacher has own child in
        class, 112
Thinking chair, 114
Threats
    over eating, 39
    you can't carry out, 81–82
    that imply a choice, 83
    working parents, 103
Throwing
    child, to relieve feelings, 122
    child, unintentionally hitting
        another, 65
    legitimate uses of, 65

Time
    child's sense of, 71
    giving child time to learn, 45
    spent nagging and scolding, 23
Toy chests, 48
Transition
    from one activity to another, 8–10
Trust
    adults destroy, 33, 115
    and lying, 58
    begins at birth, 34
    child, of adult, 31, 142
    How do we instill?, 35
    parents-teachers, 154

Values
    adults—lying, 57
    brought from home, 61
    teachers, acquired over years, 61
Violence, 66
Viorst, Judith, 129

Water play
    to relieve tension, 129
Working parents
    and communication, 144, 145
    and family meetings, 135–137
    anxiety, 101, 103
    feeling criticized, 6
    in a child care center, 109, 112
    problems of, 4, 36

About The Author

Dr. Grace Mitchell is an author, lecturer, consultant, and co-founder of a national chain of day care centers. She has had more than 50 years experience working with young children. Since 1933 she has been a pioneer of nursery school education. She has written three books on child care, received a masters degree from Harvard at age 53 and a PhD at 70 from Union Graduate School. Dr. Mitchell has three children and five grandchildren.

"*A Very Practical Guide to Discipline* may sound like a guide to punishment, but it is actually a guide to avoiding punishment. Although she encourages parents to find ways to avoid problem situations, she states that there are times when punishment is necessary. When a child infringes on the rights of another person, by hurting them or destroying property, or being deliberately rude, penalties are in order."

"The lynchpin of Mitchell's philosophy is "I AM, I CAN," which encourages self-esteem in children on the theory that an individual with a healthy self-image is better able to function in society."

"Mitchell draws on her five decades as a parent, grandparent, teacher and school administrator to look at the issues that parents face every day. She uses scores of based-on-fact anecdotes to describe the techniques she has developed for handling age-old problems. The stories she tells are sometimes humorous, sometimes sad, always insightful."

> Christine McKenna
> Lowell, Sun, Lowell, Mass.

"In an easy-to-read style, Mitchell outlines her four point plan of action: Anticipate, Hesitate, Investigate and Communicate. This and her I AM, I CAN philosophy have become measuring sticks measuring sticks for child-rearing."

> C. J. Boyer
> Las Vegas Review-Journal

"Mitchell is very much in touch with today's young children, and has a warm writing style that makes "A Very Practical Guide to Discipline" easy to read."

> Marge Cocker
> Seattle Post-Intelligencer

"A good-natured, commonsensical approach to the age-old problems of child-rearing, distilled from better than fifty years of dealing with kids."

> Jerry Carroll
> San Francisco Chronicle

"The Mitchell book is briskly written, replete with sound advice and anecdotes which help clarify and illuminate her message."

> Larry Rumley
> Seattle Times

"Dr. Mitchell's book offers a variety of down to earth techniques as a source for both parents and teachers to use while they are guiding and nurturing the lives of young children. Every school in our company has one."

> Buffy Owens
> Executive Vice President
> Palo Alto Preschools

"Dr. Mitchell doesn't preach or make us feel guilty about the mistakes we've all made with our children. Instead, true to life situations help us to really understand how positive discipline works."

"Anticipate, Hesitate, Investigate, Communicate is a plan of action that will work for parents and teachers. It will allow us, bit by bit, to develop in children the ability to be responsible for their own behavior."

> Judith Adorno
> Region Manager
> Kindercare Learning Centers

"This is an ideal book for child care teachers as well as parents. Dr. Mitchell, through many lively anecdotes gives the reader an understanding of what makes children tick. There is no simple formula or recipe for discipline. Instead, she offers flexible techniques that work. At last, a book on discipline that makes sense."

> Karen Miller
> Director of Training
> Children's World

For additional copies of *A Very Practical Guide To Discipline With Young Children* send the coupon below to TelShare Publishing Company, P.O. Box 679 Marshfield, Mass. 02050 or CALL TOLL FREE 1-800-343-9707 (617-834-8774 in Mass.)

TelShare can also offer you copies of *To Be A Trial Lawyer* by F. Lee Bailey, available in soft-cover or leather with reader's name in gold leaf and personalized inscription by F. Lee Bailey.

--------------------- cut here for mailing

TelShare Publishing Co.
P.O. Box 679, Marshfield, MA 02050
CALL TOLL FREE 1-800-343-9707. (617-834-8774 in Mass.)
Or, use this coupon. (Call for quantity discounts.)

Send me:

____ copies of *To Be A Trial Lawyer* $14.95 ea.

____ copies of the special personalized,
leather bound edition, *To Be A
Trial Lawyer* $39.95 ea.

____ copies of *A Very Practical Guide
to Discipline* $ 8.95 ea.

Add $1.00 for postage.   I have enclosed _____

_____
Please sign

_____
print your name

Form of payment (check one)

☐ check   (Make payable to
☐ money order   TelShare Publishing Company, Inc.)
☐ Mastercard
☐ Visa

_____
street, apt.

_____
city   state   zip

_____
credit card no.

_____
expiration date